From Coalpit to Pulpit

From Coalpit to Pulpit

REV KENNETH ERNEST ROACH

Crumps Barn Studio

For Sheila, my wife and companion on life's journey,
with all my love and gratitude

Crumps Barn Studio LLP
Crumps Barn, Syde, Cheltenham GL53 9PN
www.crumpsbarnstudio.co.uk

Copyright © Rev Kenneth Ernest Roach 2020

First printed 2020

The right of Rev Kenneth Ernest Roach to be identified as the author of this work has been asserted by him in accordance with the Copyright, Designs and Patents Act 1988.

All rights reserved. No part of this publication may be reproduced, stored in a retrieval system, or transmitted in any form or by any means, electronic, mechanical, photocopying, recording or otherwise, without the prior permission of the copyright owner.

Cover design by Lorna Gray © Crumps Barn Studio
Cover photograph © Rev Kenneth Ernest Roach
Photographic plates © Rev Kenneth Ernest Roach

ISBN 978-1-9998705-9-1

A note from the author

I was born into a coal miner's home, May 5 1922, and now am in my twentieth year of retirement. My life has been a journey from real poverty to relative plenty; from rural simplicities to city sophistications in Britain and America; from the religious fundamentalism of Pentecostalism to a Faith that is liberal and inter-Faith – and from a coalpit to pulpits.

It has been an unusual pilgrimage, stimulating to look back upon, rewarding to re-live and, hopefully, of interest to others. My memories may well be distorted by understatement or exaggeration but, such is the nature of the mind – sometimes all too human. Every re-write would probably tell a different story – in interpretations, if not in the record of historical facts.

The living of it has been mainly in blocks of fourteen years, and it has been a privilege to have lived through such a variety of experiences and good fortunes. The revival of memories has stirred emotions which may well have influenced judgements and, of course, the "living of these days" is still going on. But, after twenty years of retirement, an account is justified.

Ken Roach

Chapter 1

Childhood in 1920's South Wales

*M*y **earliest memory** consists of finding myself as a child sitting in the front room window of a terraced cottage in Kenfig Hill (a village between Bridgend and Portalbot in South Wales). I was waiting with my younger brother for my father to return from the Salvation Army soup kitchen with an enamel jug of pea soup, which would be our main meal for the day. It was probably the time of the coal miners' strike in 1926, and the loss of income was biting at every level. We did not feel particularly deprived, because coal mining was the only occupation available to most men – so everyone around us was in the same predicament, and there was as much mutual help as each was able to give others.

The cottage was the end house in a terrace of four on High Street. Conditions were normal in those days, but very basic by modern standards. Electricity had not yet arrived in the village, so lighting was provided by candles and oil lamps, the latter being suspended from the ceiling or attached to the walls. All our heat came from a small range which was about nine foot square and about a foot deep. It consisted of a coal fireplace and above this was a hotplate on which water could be heated and, on the right, an oven in which all our food was cooked. In the front room, there was an open fireplace which we only used on special occasions because of the cost of coal.

Our only toilet was "out the back", which meant in the back garden. Our only water supply was a tap, also outside at the back of the house. This facility often froze in the winter. The door from the living room opened directly onto the elements. The floors were of slab-stones covered with mats – usually homemade from bits of old rags. The wallpaper on the side of the stairs frequently fell off in the winter, because of the damp coming through from the 'pine-end' (the gable end) of the terraced house.

Bed warmth came from blankets and the fact that every bed usually had at least two occupants – and often more. The priority for the first person to get up in the morning was to light a fire in the grate (starting with wood), and then to boil the kettle of water for the first cup of tea. Being constantly cold in the winter was taken for granted; we didn't know any different in those days, so perhaps didn't suffer as much as these descriptions may suggest to a reader now.

Our food was basic, much of it being grown in our gardens or allotments. Four meals a day were common; breakfast, and dinner around noon – this was usually the cooked meal; then tea – which consisted of bread and butter, jam and cake and, perhaps, fruit. Our supper often consisted of leftovers from the previous meals. Indeed, the evening fry-up was often the most tasty meal of the day, and probably helped keep us warmer in bed on a cold night. Most beds were feather beds, which could be lumpy and uncomfortable; a hot water bottle was customary on cold nights, and a 'container' under the bed served for any toilet calls.

We entertained many visitors of one kind or another. These were often relatives coming for a holiday. The men slept with my father; my mother usually joined my brother and me in a three-quarter-size bed in a smaller room. On a hot summer night the inevitable discomfort of the three of us can easily be imagined. There was also a small box room with a single bed, and this often saw two lady visitors sleeping together. There was never any feelings of the inappropriate nature (by modern standards) of these arrangements. This was commonly the situation in most homes; there was no alternative. Most families had to entertain relatives or friends in this way.

The same conditions applied with we had holidays with relatives. Indeed, when my parents were married in 1919 they went on honeymoon to my father's sister in Bristol. The house, a three and a half bedroom/ shop conversion slept the husband and wife, a boy who slept in the small room off the parents' room, and two girls with another child on the way. Again no indoor toilet or central heating, and only one living room (because the front room had been converted into a butcher's shop).

I don't remember any conception of what we now call a B&B, or hotel accommodation. Almost all our holidays were taken in that house in Bristol and the cousins, visiting us for a holiday near the sea in South Wales, often brought friends as well.

During my early years I remember my father's youngest brother getting married, and the couple moving in with us – their first child being born in our home. On at least two occasions we took in male lodgers who had quarrelled with their fathers, and a young widow lived with us for years because she couldn't tolerate her mother-in-law. Not all of these lived with us at the same time, of course. Memories associated with each of these extra residents are vivid, but I don't remember feeling deprived, or that the overcrowding was unusual. On the whole, relationships were tolerable, and most people accepted the situation because they were not aware of better circumstances with which to make a comparison.

I remember one lodger who was trying to learn to play the violin. In spite of a crowded living room, Archie Evans would prop up some music on the chest of drawers and screech away on his fiddle – he showed no concern for how his efforts were interfering with people's conversations, or how he was simply setting our teeth on edge.

He was a member of the household, he needed to practice his hobby, and he just had to do it where and how he could. I don't even remember anyone objecting, or any undue tensions; I think we were immune, accepted the limitations of such conditions, and simply got on with what we had to do.

My Parents

My father grew up in the Forest of Dean. He was one of twelve children living in a small terraced cottage. They could give accounts of many children sleeping in the same bed; having to grow their own vegetables in large gardens; keeping pigs and chickens for meat; obtaining fruit from their own apple and pear orchards. Such overcrowded living was a preparation for the conditions he experienced when he married my mother, as well as providing plenty of occupation for their energies as they created their own means of living.

In their late teenage or early adulthood, for various reasons, many of the children my father grew up with migrated to South Wales – probably to find work in the coal mines, travelling there on their bicycles. There are no records of any of this, but I remember snippets of conversations, and impressions, which comprise a hazy picture of family backgrounds which may or may not be accurate.

My mother's parents came from Cornwall and Windsor. Grandfather Hopkins was a tailor by profession and a Primitive Methodist by conviction. He was a devout and lovable man. His boyhood was near Barnstable, and he often told of his very early days on a farm. He established a tailoring business in Port Talbot, South Wales, working in a small back room, making suits to order, and doing alterations for all the clothier shops in the town. One of my mother's sisters became his assistant for the whole of his life.

My maternal grandmother was a tall, slight, hardworking woman who brought up three girls and a boy. She made delicious home-made soups of beef tea and created a home that was always comfortable and resourceful – leaving me with very happy memories of my visits there. She was a devout Anglican but attended the Methodist Church for the sake of the children growing up, only to return to her Church of England roots later. She made incomparable fishcakes and had simple remedies for every ailment.

The house in St Mary Street was purchased for £107 in 1901, and further improvements had cost another

£40. There was a strength and quietness in the home and life there was restful, and yet encouraged creative play. There was always plenty to eat and I spent many happy Christmases there, as well as frequent weekends. My mother would take me on Friday afternoons, and my grandmother returned me home on Monday – a journey of about 7 miles.

I don't remember my grandfather ever visiting our home; though I am not aware of any disaffection between my parents and grandparents. However, I'm sure my grandparents must have felt their eldest daughter could have done better for herself than marrying a coal miner and moving into a crowded village cottage.

My mother left school to do 'Gentleman's service', common in those days; being of bigger build than her sisters, she frequently described herself as a 'big lump of a girl'. There were overtones in her self-description which suggested a poor opinion of herself, or maybe a sense of being the least loved and more 'put upon' than the other children.

The boy was, of course, the favourite; one sister worked all her life in a nearby grocer shop; the other stayed at home to work with Grandfather; both remained single.

How my parents met, I have no idea. Kenfig Hill is seven miles from Port Talbot; there was no independent transport; I know of no social interests or concerns that might have brought them into contact, or how long they had known each other before getting married.

My mother moved into the Roach family cottage, where my parental grandmother was also living with her youngest son Harvey. The old lady died suddenly, and soon Harvey married and moved into the front room. Their first child was born there a year or so after my birth, to be joined by a brother for me about the same time.

I remember a story my mother used to tell about cousin Cyril going missing – only to be informed by me, "Oh, I've locked 'Spider' in the pantry!" It appears that 'Spider' was a quiet, uncomplaining lad who accepted his treatment without protest.

Such are some of my early recollections of home and family life. I do not remember any of the friction or serious frustrations that one might expect from overcrowding in such primitive conditions. There must have been some, of course, but such as they were left me with no unhappy memories. The sequence of events is hazy, but about this time Harvey, Bessie, and son Cyril moved out. Haydn, my brother, was born almost two years after my birth, and then a third boy called Bernard came a little later.

Unfortunately, Bernard died before he was three, and I remember some relationships with him – also the little white coffin that rested for a few days just inside the front room door. On the day of the funeral, Haydn and I were sent to Port Talbot to spend the day with our grandparents. In those days, death was more common among the young, and funeral processions could be seen marching down the road towards the cemetery. Coffins were borne on the shoulders of the bearers, and appropriate songs of Faith were sung by the mourners.

Among my earliest memories are those of two younger brothers. The younger, Bernard, as a devout little soul who loved "to play at meetings", and to imitate some of the more dramatic preachers – though he was not three years old when he died of a bowel condition. One such preacher was our uncle Harvey who, when making a point, would rotate his hand in a series of circles and then extend his forefinger with a forward thrust to emphasise the point he was making. Bernard would go through the motions and say, "Uncle Harvey goes like this!"

Haydn was the middle child. He was full of life and very intelligent. As a boy , he could read very quickly, and remember what he had read. For instance, I recall him reading a big book in a short time, to the disbelief of my grandfather – who decided to question him on the details of the story, only to find that Haydn could answer all the questions! I don't recall his achievements at school – perhaps these were limited because, though very intelligent, he also loved athletics and was essentially more light-hearted than myself.

After school, Haydn worked for a while with our father in the colliery but decided that was not for him – so he became a farm labourer, living in the farm house, earning fifteen shillings a week, and working from dawn till dusk. He later transferred to another farm where he worked for about ten years, during which time he married and began raising a fine family of seven children. When he needed more money than the farm would pay, he transferred to the railway – where he remained for the rest of his life.

Haydn was always more adventurous than me and broke the family pattern by purchasing a motorcycle whilst a teenager (and, later, a car). To my mother's frequent injunction, "Now take care of the old motor-bike!" Haydn would reply with a laugh, "Now don't worry mother; I'd rather be ten minutes late down here, then ten years too soon up there!" He would also say with a laugh, "I know I'm doing seventy miles an hour when every nut and bolt is rattling!"

Haydn was adept at writing humorous poetry and melodies. He turned his hand to several instruments and was a member of a Quintet that composed most of its own songs, pleasing many congregations with their contributions to the worship.

One of his funny poems was written on the occasion

of our buying a pair of hair clippers, and my starting to cut the hair of Hayden and our father – as well as a few boys in the neighbourhood. The poem began:

> *Ken started cutting hair, but for him we didn't care,*
> *Because he wasn't very fair with our hair.*
> *But we sat in the chair, and took the dare,*
> *Then sent up a prayer for our sweet ole hair.*

It was quite a lengthy poem which I could never read through for laughing.

In these and other respects we were so different. Haydn has remained in the Pentecostal Church and risen to top ranks of local leadership. At the same time, he could cause much merriment describing things that happened which were rather silly and irreverent. Here he offered a good mixture of basic seriousness with a continuing sense of humour – which he still has. His house, unlike mine, is always open for anyone who wishes to drop in. A cup of tea, a Welsh cake, and a leisurely chat are always available. When my mother could no longer live alone, Hayden and Ruth took her into their home and gave her all the help she needed until she died at the age of ninety-six.

Returning to my childhood, I went to school at the age of four. It was the local primary school, where 'the three R's' were the basic education. It was walking distance from home, and we returned for lunch after the morning session. It included physical exercises as well as time for playing games (mainly rugby football). Singing sessions were also part of the curriculum. We were encouraged to read and discuss – so there was a general culture, though academic depth in any subject was not available.

My school memories are generally happy, though there were difficulties because of the very public expressions of our Pentecostal religion and its in-built exclusiveness. We never went to a cinema, so could not share what the other children were talking about. We didn't have a radio, so didn't know the songs most children were singing. We didn't play around with girls, so were regarded as odd – and we felt it.

However, because we were being indoctrinated with the idea that we were *superior* (that we had the light, everyone else being in the dark; that we were the saved, they were the sinners), there were compensations for our feelings of being ostracised. We were really sandwiched between two worlds – the social world, and the 'Kingdom of God'.

Our father had made all this very public. Every year, the village hall held a carnival, with the bands and youth organisations parading the streets on a Saturday afternoon. Father felt a 'Call' to use such an opportunity to witness to his Faith. He arranged for a banner to be made from an old shop blind, about two feet by three, and erected this on a wooden pole. On one side, in large letters, was the text "Prepare to meet thy God". Behind, were the words "The Scriptures cannot be broken". As the procession began its march, father stepped out from the shop door and marched ahead of the parade with his banner held high. He stayed in his position for the whole of the march.

Everyone knew who he was. The children in school also knew who we were. On the following Monday morning in class I heard one boy saying to another, "It's a pity for the Roach boys, but it isn't their fault; it's their father's."

At the end of the school days I have to report a bitter memory. We arrived at the last Friday. We were looking forward to the celebrations of the final afternoon when prizes and gifts were often distributed. We went home as usual for lunch, only to be told by my mother, "You are not going back to school. You must stay home to help with housework."

I couldn't believe what I was hearing. I cried, pleaded, but she was adamant. So instead of celebrating the last session at school with teachers and friends, I was at home scrubbing floors and polishing furniture. Seventy years have since passed but, rightly or wrongly, the memory is still pointed.

Perhaps to describe this episode is unfortunate and may be too uncharitable. There may well have been visiting preachers coming for the weekend, and mother certainly held the 'men of God' in very high esteem.

As for herself, she often described her ideal as being "a mother in Israel" – whatever that may have meant in her mind. Marrying my father, she had to make major adjustments in housekeeping and lifestyle. His was a big family, and many of them were now living in the vicinity. Though they were almost all very religious, they each had a different emphasis and affiliation, so the inevitable arguments were often quite disturbing. My father was, in her words, "never much company".

Then, at some time, my parents became involved in a charismatic movement which began in cottage meetings, these were held only four doors away in the house of my father's sister. My mother talked of creeping around during these meetings to listen at the window what was going on. Later, they too became involved, so that cottage meetings were held in our house. We had to borrow chairs from neighbours so that a group of perhaps ten or twelve could be accommodated in our living room.

The meetings consisted of spontaneous prayers, readings from the Bible (with expositions), the Pentecostal feature of 'speaking in tongues' (with 'interpretation') and sometimes, prophecies. The participants aspired to being filled with the Holy Ghost as well as being born-again Christians, and they felt they were superior to every other 'nominal' Christian (as well as non-Christians). It was all very heady stuff, and may have helped to compensate for the poverty and social deprivation which were common in their everyday lives.

My parents later became involved with the Apostolic variety of Pentecostalism, and such was their dedication that the Biblical standard of Tithes was accepted. This meant that, without question, a tenth of all their income went to the Church (that was the Lord's portion as of right) – plus a generous *offering* from the nine-tenths that were left. These convictions almost certainly helped to make my mother what she was, and to determine her priorities. If such a 'man of God' was coming to stay with us for the weekend – then it was more important that the house should be clean and the meals prepared, than that her son should spend his last Friday afternoon in school. "Even though it would be the last, so what?"

Further Afield

*A*t **the age of twelve** I found a morning job, delivering milk with the local farmer. These were the days of a horse-drawn 'dray', with the milk in different sized 'jacks' (containers that might hold ten gallons down to one gallon).

We carried the milk in the small container of about half a gallon, and measured it out in pint and half-pint measures. It meant knocking at doors and measuring the milk into the family jug. Halfway round, I had to go to another farm to replenish my supplies. This was heavy work, involving a walk about half a mile over a railway bridge, carrying about two gallons. I started about 7.15am and, on weekdays, left the round about 9am to arrive at school in time for the opening at 9.30am. I was paid 2/6d per week (twelve and a half pence nowadays!)

About this time I also began music lessons on piano and organ. These cost exactly half of my weekly wage (so a comparison with today's standards can be calculated). My aunt Bessie was limited in her ability to lead effective singing on the Mission organ, so it was hoped I would replace her – and this is what eventually happened. We had acquired a small harmonium that we kept in the front room. On winter evenings this had to be carried into the living room for me to practice. The family was so keen for me to become the church organist that all such inconveniences were gladly accepted. Later I discovered a fourteen-stop organ in Bridgend Market for £7.0.0d, which was purchased and installed permanently in the front room, and on which I hopefully matured somewhat as an organist. When I left home some years later, the organ was given to the Mission, where it was used to lead the hymn singing for many years.

My father was a coalminer, lame from an accident sustained whilst young. He was very limited, having had little formal education. I believe he went down the coal mines at about the age of eleven. His reading was almost entirely in the Bible and Apostolic monthly publication called the *Riches of Grace.* He was regarded in the Mission as a prophet of God, and one who could therefore 'interpret' when the unknown tongues were uttered. He was also Secretary and Treasurer, which indicates either his abilities – or the lack of such in the other members of the group.

Needless to say, our home life was dominated by the religious factor, and family requirements were secondary to the religious priorities. I don't remember any gifts or celebrations of our birthdays, or at Christmas. Natural affection was secondary to religious duties, and observance of meetings occupied most of our leisure time.

Later, the group moved out of the 'cottage meeting' venue to an old garage down a rough lane. Later still it moved again – into a football hut. There were prayer meetings every Tuesday, Thursday, and Saturday evening, plus an extra Missionary meeting on the first Monday of every month.

The meetings lasted about two hours and were punctuated with hymns, spontaneous prayers. Scripture readings and exposition, plus fairly frequent 'speaking in tongues' and prophesying. Many verses of hymns were sung repeatedly with devout enthusiasm, and I remember at least one occasion when we sang through a hymn – only to repeat the last verse and sing the hymn again from the last verse to the first. Any member of the congregation could announce a hymn at any time, repeat a chorus or verse, or give a personal testimony or exposition.

Whatever happened was assumed to be under the

direction of the Holy Spirit, and therefore not subject to human judgement or criticism. I have known a man preach for a hour and twenty-five minutes (all attributed to the inspiration of the holy Ghost) with unflagging zeal for his message. On one occasion, I remember my mother scolding me because I had looked bored stiff at the meeting – to which I replied, "I was!"

Such was the intensely religious context of my early childhood. I think I tried to share the idealism and remember when very young going through the motions of "being saved". I remember forcing myself to stand up in a testimony meeting and saying, "I accept the Lord Jesus Christ as my personal Saviour, and by His Grace I mean to go on." The meeting responded with "Amens" and "Hallelujahs", and thereafter it was felt that Ken had been saved.

However, on reflection, I'm sure that was more an attempt to be part of the group and to be accepted than a sincere expression of personal conviction. Personal dissatisfaction and criticisms were increasing and I was not really a happy member – though because of the complete family context I certainly tried hard to be one of them.

My father, in his behaviour, could be a mixture of

religious dedication and lack of sensitivity to feelings or appropriate action. When only in my first year at school, I came home and repeated something I had been taught (or sang a song we had learned). My father was indignant and said, "Tell your teacher not to teach you such rubbish!"

The next day I went straight to Miss Blatchford and said, "My father told me to tell you not to teach us such rubbish!"

I can still see her – a tall, dignified person looking down at me and, shocked, simply saying "Kenneth Roach!"

On another occasion, we were on a Sunday School treat to a favourite spot in the countryside called Merthyr Mawr. It was a delightful area among sand hills, streams, and an old castle. On arrival at the castle we boys used to climb back on the open lorry that had brought us and go back to another area about half a mile away where there was a swinging bridge. On this occasion my mother was not on the trip, or she might have known we had done it on previous outings. My father missed us, learned what we had done, and set out to meet us to teach us a lesson.

He was very angry. On seeing us, about half way back to the castle ground – he went into the hedge, broke off a branch with a stem about as thick as a finger, and gave Haydn and me a severe beating in front of our friends. This took place on a Sunday School outing. Perfectly innocent and harmless behaviour. A week later, I could still show a thick weal across the back of my knee, noticeable because we all wore short trousers in those days;

Of course, it was more acceptable then for children to be corrected by such punishment and, in addition to this, Bible-based Christians knew the proverb "Spare the rod and spoil the child".

My uncle Charlie, also a leader in a Pentecostal mission, would show visitors to his home two straps handing on the wall above his fireplace. One was about an inch across, which he use on his children for a minor misdemeanour. On the other side was a much heavier belt with a large buckle that was used when it was felt that heavier punishment was warranted. I remember the grin on his face while he was talking about his belts and how he used them; even then, I knew there was something wrong somewhere between the claims of religious superiority and the lack we children felt of any genuine affection or regard for our total welfare.

Many of these memories were obviously not pleasant, and may cloud my judgement. However, they are part of the story – but other considerations should also be taken into account. Life in general was hard and insecure. There were few creature comforts, especially by today's standards. Our parent had a very limited education, and corporal punishment of children was generally accepted. Even policemen and teachers were allowed to give a child a 'clip across the ear' or a good caning in school.

If mother felt she could not give the appropriate beating to a misbehaving child, her threat was, "You wait till your father comes home; he'll give you what for!" The threat was real, and beatings with hand or stick were common, as well as being sent to bed early.

In the context of poverty, insecurity, limited education and a rough background themselves, the behaviour of our parents must be judged with some sympathy and much understanding. I have often said that my parents lived fully from what they had to the highest standards that they knew – and you can't ask much more than that. The economic and social context left little room for emotional sensitivities; it was the general situation in the nation as well as in our local communities and families.

However, if a person is looking back over his past, in order better to understand himself in the present, then all the factors must be taken into consideration and analysed. One's adult reaction to circumstances, and the handling of all kinds of problems, must be seen with the psychological tendencies from heredity as well as the acquired dispositions and influences.

We are all very complex creatures. It has been said, "to

know all is to forgive all". This is one of the consolations of religion – that God, the righteous judge, will have full knowledge of everything that has made us what we are, and will sow love and mercy in his judgements.

As to the right way to rear children, I don't think any intelligent person will claim to be a perfect parent. How can we be, when we have each been subject to many imperfections in our own upbringings, with the consequent quirks in our characters over which we may have a distorted understanding and, therefore, limited responsibility or control?

So, this review of my home and school years is a mixture. We did have wonderful surrounding countryside to enjoy. We were able to roam freely with little danger of molestation. We played football or cricket, enjoying plenty of space and fresh air. We had a farm where we enjoyed helping on special occasions such as harvest-gathering. We were only cycling distances from the sea and lovely beaches – as well as a rocky coastline.

On the whole, our advantages balanced our disadvantages – and I regard myself as fortunate in the family and community environment in which I found myself. The hardships may have given impetus to personal development. Many a person has, upon reflection, felt that their difficulties may had spurred them to higher levels of success in lifestyles, as well as skills. In any case, each of us has a challenge in the 'pack of cards' that life has given us, and the privilege to do what we can with them – allowing for the limitations we each have to contend with.

Chapter 2

Coal Miner

I **completed my schooling** in July 1936; then arose the question of employment. There were only two options – either to become a farm labourer, or a coal miner.

Adult colliers needed boys to work with them so, in August, I went to the coal mine as an assistant to my father. We worked in Pentre Colliery, one of three mines in the area. These had been worked for many years, and the coalfaces were very deep – about three miles underground.

Some coal pits go directly into the ground, and then fan out along the coal seam. Our colliery was a 'slant', which descends into the mountain at about a one inch in four gradient. The first slant went down about a mile, then we descended another in a different direction for half a mile. There followed an eight-hundred-yard ride in trams, on a level, only to descend again for almost a mile, eventually coming to our 'heading'. Off this we dug our coal from what was called a stall, five yards wide. Between each heading of about sixty yards, the colliers extracted coal from a seam three feet thick and on a slope.

This meant that all our work was done on our knees in a perpetually bent position. The adult miner dug the coal with a mandrill (pick) and shovelled it into a low wooden cart, holding about half a ton, which was then lowered to the heading shaft where the boy shovelled it into a steel tram – roughly a ton of coal. The trams supplying five or six parallel stalls would be drawn by horses, and the 'man and boy' would need to produce about six trams of coal per shift to make a basic living. If the coalface was hard, it was difficult to make a minimum wage. Alternatively, if the seam at the point had been subjected to some crushing from below, then the work would be easier, and more coal would be produced.

Conditions were difficult. It took about an hour and a half to reach the coalface. The height in which you worked was about thirty-six inches; your light was a candle, or a carbide lamp; and the air was always full of dust. If you worked on the heading, where some ground had to be dug up to allow enough height for horses and trams, you were in danger of contracting silicosis from the silica rock, while the coal dust caused pneumoconiosis.

Coal dust eventually occupied twenty-six percent of my father's lungs, and this inevitably hastened his death at the age of sixty-eight.

Apart from extracting coal from the stall, each collier had to open an airway into each of the adjoining stalls, about seven yards up to the stall and parallel to the heading. This system of airways connected to the surface, where the largest building housed the powerful fan. Air was thereby extracted from the lowest point in the mine, causing a steady stream to be drawn down the main slant and through the whole system.

It is impossible for me to provide further details of these airways, and how the flow of air was directed, but this was the method by which we were able to breathe at that depth and in such an accumulation of dust. Needless to say, lung diseases were widespread; many a miner died young, simply unable to breathe.

My accident

*A*ccidents **were common,** and so were frequent deaths – caused by stones falling from the roof. There were other dangers, of course, in the restricted and dark conditions. Even when a badly injured miner was brought to the surface, or even a man killed, I never remember any time when the men refused to return to their work. They simply needed the money, it was part of the employment, and it was taken for granted that serious or fatal accidents happened. My father lost a brother in such an accident and, at the age of fifteen, I myself fractured a leg from a stone falling out of the roof.

Facial injuries were common from the ground pressures which crushed the coal and caused explosions; these were called pounces. Coal would suddenly explode in the miner's face, extinguishing his light, and causing wounds from which the coal was often not fully extracted. This meant that the skin healed over the wounds, leaving a black mark; most miners had many such scars over their faces. Unless injuries were quite serious, miners accepted this as part of the job; usually no days were lost. In spite of the facial wounds, they simply carried on.

When such a 'pounce' stretched me over the ground, a stone of about twenty pounds fell out of the roof and fractured my ankle. I was put in a tram and sent to the surface, after which I had about six weeks recuperating – with a very small weekly sum for compensation. This happened at about 10.40am; from the coal mine I was taken first to a doctor, and then home by ambulance. There were no telephones to inform my mother of the accident, or to warn her of my early return. Hospitalisation was not even considered to be necessary.

After the visit to the doctor, my father asked the ambulance driver to pull up a little below our house so he could warn my mother. On arrival, mother came out of the house, looking concerned. My father started to tell her, "Ken has had an accident …" to which she replied, "Yes, I know. It happened at twenty to eleven. I've lit a fire in the front room and brought a bed downstairs."

I simply report a vivid memory but can't explain her remarks. If Mother had been asked how she knew, I'm sure she would say that the Lord had told her. Whatever we may think of this, such mystic communications are not uncommon – and are not always in a religious context.

Recently an American soldier, sailing to Iraq, was waking in his bunk only to be greeted by an officer with some bad news. The boy's father had died unexpectedly in the night.

"Yes, I know," replied the boy, "he came to me in a dream and said 'Goodbye'."

Many a mother and wife of men serving overseas have felt an intuition that something had happened to their loved one. A subsequent official notification confirmed that death had occurred at exactly the time of the intuition.

We have no rational explanation for such experiences, but they do occur. We live in a profoundly mysterious universe where there are sometimes communications which are inexplicable, but utterly convincing to those who receive them.

After the arrival home I had to wash myself in a zinc bath, before beginning a three-week period in bed – which I enjoyed very much. Only a few days before the accident I had enrolled in an evening class to learn Pitman's shorthand. While convalescing, I not only enjoyed visits from friends and relatives, but also had plenty of time to teach myself from the textbook that I'd acquired only a few evenings before.

I was also able to read into the night, not having to worry about getting up in the morning. I wanted to learn shorthand in order that I could record messages heard in the Mission. After all, they were regarded as messages from God, so it was well worth learning a skill to record them for future meditation.

It may be of interest to repeat that there was never a question of compensation from my employer for the accident. Following my recovery, I worked with my father for about two years – when my brother took my place as father's 'boy'. I became an assistant to a very elderly coal miner who was at least in his mid-seventies. Haydn, however, did not like the work – so left to become a farm labourer on nearby Pentre Farm.

I, too, did not like working on the coalface – so took another job as a haulage driver. This meant working in an engine room where a huge drum with a steel rope lowered and raised the trams on their many ways to the surface. In this form of employment, though still deep underground, I was able to read books under electric light (when the engine was not in use). As a haulage driver I must have read hundreds of books over the course of about seven years. All this reading helped to lay a good foundation for future thought and spiritual development.

From this work I was invited to be trained as a rope-smith and, as such, finished my colliery employment. This entailed being on hand to repair steel ropes of five-eighths to one inch thick, which meant splicing them together after a complete break or ravel.

Once I had joined my father in the coal mine, and especially when Hayden also came down the pit, there was a problem about the necessary bathing process. We only had limited hot water, which was heated on the stove. We carried the zinc bath into the kitchen to wash ourselves in front of the living room fire. The bath, carried in from outside, contained perhaps two inches of cold water; hot water was then added. One of us knelt by the bath, washed the head and top half, and then dried himself with a towel. The second man would then repeat the process – by which time the water was like black ink. The first man would then kneel in the bath, and wash the bottom half of his body – followed by the second man who would again repeat the process.

Sometimes we were all three on the same 'shift', so each had to bath in the same water (supplemented periodically, of course, by more hot water). When we were on different shifts, the procedure had to be done at eight-hour intervals, which made it particularly difficult for my mother who always worked hard to keep the house clean and tidy. On summer days, especially Saturdays, we were expected to bath in a small out-house where we could hardly turn around – much less bath properly; but at least we didn't spoil all the housework done in preparation for the weekend and, possibly, the entertaining of visiting preachers.

Books

*D*uring these years I continued to be an avid reader and spent as much time as I could on my own – thinking, reading or writing my meditations. I was keen to understand psychology, philosophy and of course, religion. Many coal miners were also intellectuals, though having little formal education. Amongst coal miners I developed a curiosity about Shakespeare, classical music, and the ancient philosophers. In my teens, I was reading Aristotle, Plato, and other thinkers. I found that they too had ideas on religion and how life should be lived, hence I didn't feel so guilty about such matters – though I could not discuss any of this with family or friends in the Mission.

I did have a non-religious cousin, Jack Roach, who was older than me and took an interest in my improving education. He too was a reader and introduced me to the library of the Miners' Welfare Institute, as well as to general books.

Another cousin, Eric Painter, a regular churchgoer, introduced me to more liberal religious reading. The first book he gave me was called *In Tune with the Infinite* by Ralph Waldo Trine. One day I found a list of second-hand books for sale, among which were two titles which made an instant appeal. One was *The Manhood of the Master* and the other *The meaning of Prayers* – by an American named Harry Emerson Fosdick. I knew nothing of the author, nor his particular theology, but I sent for the books. So began a wider and deeper exploration into religious and Christian interpretation.

Thereafter, whenever Eric and I were together in a town, we eagerly looked for bookstores – with a top priority of finding more titles by Fosdick. We found many, for he had written over twenty books, and we devoured these as a hungry man consumes a tasty meal.

Fosdick was a Liberal thinker and I realised that the interpretations of his work would not be welcome in my Fundamentalist circles, and so was discreet in my communications about the discoveries. At this time I had begun local preaching in the Mission, and was often part of the Bible Class discussions. I know my friends suspected that I was drifting from the 'straight and narrow'. Nevertheless, I could often quote Biblical texts to support my unfamiliar views – so my contributions attracted much interest.

I was soon regarded as an 'odd one out', yet I kept my place in the community and, in my late teens, was invited to become a church officer in a nearby Assembly at Cornelly – about three miles away. My readings in the books by Fosdick, and personal reflections, caused me to drift further and further away from the charismatic ethos – though there was never any question of my breaking away from the Mission. After all, it was the hub of our family life; I was known by all our friends as an active member, and it was assumed that basically I was still 'sound in the Faith' (though in some way different from most others). I knew enough of their positions to discuss their ideas, whilst increasingly keeping my own growing convictions to myself.

I was also beginning to make other explorations. Most of my life was spent within the boundaries of the church, coal mine and village. One day I determined to be adventurous and took a coach to Cardiff (about twenty-six miles away), feeling very grown-up and mature. Whilst looking round some shops I saw a shirt on display in a window which attracted my fancy. I asked myself, "Why not buy it? I am earning money now."

I entered the shop and requested the blue and white shirt in the window. The shop assistant said, "What size, sir?"

"Size? What has size got to do with it? I simply want to buy that shirt!"

The assistant was the soul of tact and quietly said, "Sir, if you will loosen your tie, I will look inside your collar and tell you your size."

So I made my first independent purchase, probably near my twentieth birthday. Hitherto, Mother had bought all our clothes; we were very much influenced by her choices and decisions.

Another personal such breakaway from family control came when a local dramatic group, of which cousin Jack was a member, decided to perform a Shakespeare play in Cefn Cribbwr, about a mile away. I said I wanted to see it. My parents were aghast; theatre, cinema – even radio – were "of the world", and not for born again Christians.

The evening for decision came. Mother pleaded with me "to resist temptation." I began the walk towards Cefn and, on the top of the hill, looked back. Mother was standing by the house, obviously trying to will my return.

I hesitated, felt the 'pull' both ways, but eventually continued the journey and saw the performance of *As You Like It*.

I don't remember enjoying the evening or understanding the play, but I had taken a stand. I had thereby asserted more of my independence, and somehow that felt right and good, in spite of the guilt and regret at causing pain to Mother.

Independence

The outward appearance of life continued. I was a rope-smith in the colliery. I attended meetings and participated in some leadership. But inwardly the gap was widening, and although I knew mother had prayed that I would become an Apostolic Pastor, I was sure this was not for me. I couldn't accept the narrow Fundamentalism, nor the charismatic evidences of so-called "being baptised in the Holy Spirit".

However, at that time, and in that place, there were still no real alternative to these forms of worship – so I carried on with living the double life of seeming to be part of the group, yet increasingly becoming very different.

These were the war years, but there was no question of call-up for military duties. Coal was needed for the ships, and conscientious objectors to the war could elect to work in the coal mine as an alternative.

Though drifting from my Pentecostal ideas and practices, I remained a serious idealist. I still have notes to myself dated 10 September 1947, written while sitting alone on rocks at Porthcawl. I wanted to know the truth about life as reflected in the world's philosophy and poetry, as well as in religion. I determined to read all the great books I could obtain, and try to digest them. I wanted to be able to appreciate classical music, and other forms of art. I also wanted to be a gardener, creating beauty, as well as organic food, and to be able to see more clearly the handiwork of God in all creation. I am almost embarrassed to read the great ambitions I had at that age; yet I can also see that a pattern was forming for my future which has helped to shame my whole development.

Towards the end of this period came an unexpected turning point. Cousin Jack suggested I attend a summer school with him in Coleg Harlech, North Wales.

Coleg Harlech was a Workers' Education Association College for the further education of the working man who had not benefitted from an academic education. We went; and enjoyed the week of lectures and discussions, and the general atmosphere of such an institution of learning.

It was suggested that I consider spending a year in

residence. I said I would think about it but wanted to do some preparatory reading first. The Bursar replied, "You come here and let us guide your reading."

Whilst being attracted to the prospect I was aware of my family context, and my status in the coal mine, so I decided against the move – though with some hesitation.

A few weeks later; I was accused by the manager of the colliery of something I had not done. I was angry at his attitude as well as the accusations and, on leaving the colliery, said to myself "Blow that man, and the job; I'll spend a year in Coleg Harlech!" With no more hesitation I applied for a place, was accepted, and joined the College community at the beginning of Winter term 1949.

Coleg Harlech

*T*here was no entrance examinations, very low fees, and no certificates at the end of the studies. The idea was that you improved your general knowledge in a variety of subjects, and then returned to your village and tried to help other adults with similar ambitions – for example, by offering evening classes. My cousin Jack (who was a Socialist) had spent the previous year in the Collage, and he subsequently offered evening classes in Economics and Social History.

I opted for studies in Philosophy, Psychology and English Literature. Thus began my break from the coal pit, and a major step in my journey to the pulpit.

Regarding the decisive point of the break, I have often wondered whether my altercation with the Colliery manager was a coincidence or another example of

Shakespeare's insight – *"There's a destiny which shapes our ends, rough hew them how we will."*

Who knows for sure?

Some of us can look back and be amazed at apparently casual 'happenings' that caused us to turn corners and travel in an entirely different direction. My unfolding story will show other such turnings and confirm my conviction that I was destined for the Pulpit Ministry. Such a conviction has certainly helped in the difficult times, as well as being an inspiration at all times.

One such 'incident' was a letter early in 1949 inviting me to preach at the Apostolic Whitsun Convention in Cardiff. I was not the first choice, but one of the speakers had been taken ill and someone decided I could fill the vacant position. My Liberal tendencies obviously did not worry the person who invited me (or perhaps he didn't know!). However, it was at this Convention that I met Sheila, my future wife. Yet another unplanned occasion that resulted in major changes … that are still going on!

Chapter 3

A Turning Point

Coleg Harlech was a major turning, in many different ways. It offered a vast change of scenery – from the poverty and limitations of the village in South Wales to the mountains and sea views on the Merionethshire coast. The college nestled on the side of a hill with Snowdon to the right (about twenty miles distant), mountains behind, and overlooking the sea only half a mile away.

I was fortunate to be given a room at the front of the building with a balcony. Here, when the weather allowed, I spent hours reading. Though I shared the room with three other students, we all got on well. The community life was stimulating, consisting of about sixty resident students – some from overseas (one of my roommates was a German).

There was a good variety of subjects available, from general culture to economics. Morning assembly was devotional, with a liberal emphasis – the readings being more often from literature than the Bible. Students took part as they wished. Lectures occupied the morning and evening sessions; some work in the gardens during afternoons was expected once a week.

On Sundays I attended the local Methodist church, or took a picnic and spent the day alone on the mountain to the rear of the college. We arranged a group to climb Snowdon, the highest peak in the Welsh mountain ranges. We organised a cricket team that played against neighbouring sides but, on the whole, weekends were free for students to do as they liked.

Characteristically, I usually went off on my own – enjoying the mountain scenery, reading books, writing meditations at leisure, or enjoying a bathe in the sea. It was a complete contrast to the crowded, often suffocating, life of Kenfig Hill; the months passed all too quickly.

Following my introduction to Sheila, I began a correspondence with her from Harlech; it recorded my intellectual stimulations as much as my developing affection for her. Some letters, I remember, would be about twenty pages in length – and in my best handwriting, obviously designed to make a good impression! I remember buying a Christmas present for 1949 – a book of poetry which she still has, duly inscribed.

During this period, I was encouraged to apply for entrance to some kind of Higher Learning Institution, and wrote a long essay on Plato's theory of education in *The Republic*. I still have this, though it did not gain me a place.

Most of the students returned to their homes and offered fellow workers a chance to share in their educational privileges. A small percentage went on to university, and others to different forms of employment – of which I was one.

Again, this turning point was the result of an incident, or 'happening', or the 'guiding Hand'. The college was visited by Mr Robin Johns, the Director of Social Studies in Swansea University. Students who were interested in joining him in the Social Science Department there could be interviewed at leisure over a weekend. I felt no interest in this and, in any case, the word 'science' was anathema to my spiritual upbringing.

It must have been a wet Saturday afternoon, and I was reading in the college library. A friend came in, saw me, and said "Why don't you go and talk to Mr Jones; he's a nice chap, and there's no obligation."

I replied that I was not interested. Eric Hinton was persistent and, after a while, I decided there really was nothing to lose, so I went for an interview.

Mr Jones was cordial, enthusiastic about his social concerns, and convincing about my suitability in training for social work. I began to see that such an occupation might be a way of serving God among needy people. I knew I could not respond to any such 'Call' in the *Pentecosta*l ministry. I sat the entrance examination, and was duly invited to a place in the newly-formed Social Science Department in the University of Wales in Swansea.

My parents didn't like the idea of my studying any form of science but they, too accepted that it may well lead to 'good works' among people in need and, therefore, at least a form of spiritual ministry. So I returned to the colliery for three months, and then resigned from the coal-pit to become a full-time student for some kind of social service when I qualified.

University

*T*he **University course** was for two years, during which time we studied Social History in Britain, Economics, and Psychology, etc. We also had to have practical experience in at least six kinds of social institutions. These consisted of a children's home, a prison, approved schools for difficult youths, and the Assistance Board – which was the social services' safety net below which no-one was supposed to fall. It was all good experience with my specialising in Child Care. For the first year I lived with my aunts in Port Talbot – and then took lodgings with a lady in Swansea, within walking distance of the College.

During these years, my relationship with Sheila matured. We spent much time in each other's homes, and realised that our futures were to be together.

At the end of my studies came the question of future work; a potential job was open in the Children's Department of Cardiff. Mr Jones called me into his office and said he thought I should apply for it. He then suggested I should be ready for appointment at the end of the course, but thought it would be helpful if I was married. He said I should do that as soon as possible. I pleaded that I did not have good enough clothes, to which he replied, "Don't be so silly man – you only need a new tie!"

After discussion with her parents, Sheila agreed to a very simple and hastily-arranged wedding during the Easter break; we spent the honeymoon of two weeks in Bournemouth.

The job in Cardiff did not materialise, but we took temporary residence in Sheila's home pending the finding of permanent work. I worked as a labourer on a nearby building site while we watched advertisements for suitable employment.

Suddenly, one day, Sheila appeared on the site waving a letter – which was a reply to one of my applications. There was a vacancy in Bournemouth Children's Department for a Boarding-Out Officer, and I was invited to a short-list and subsequent interview.

We were excited at the prospect, but not optimistic.

Howe could an ex-coal miner be welcomed in upper class Bournemouth? We even arranged to occupy the house of a family friend in Bournemouth so that, after the interview, we could have a week's holiday – with the travelling expenses paid.

I was one of about six in the short-list and was even more pessimistic about my chances when I saw their briefcases – presumably full of references, qualifications and previous experience in the field. I simply had my Social Science Diploma, rolled up in my hand. I don't remember much about the interview, but I do remember waiting for the verdict – and being almost shocked when a smiling gentleman came into the room, looked at the other applicants and said, "I'm sorry, but Mr Roach has been appointed."

Sheila and I immediately telephoned the news to her parents, and arranged to return home on the Monday. Before doing this, I purchased a second-hand motor cycle and we found a furnished apartment in Stafford Road.

It was opposite the Juvenile Court, where I would spend each Monday afternoon for the next four years.

It was all heady stuff and emotionally demanding, but the Council wanted the worker to start as soon as possible, so we made the move – thus beginning yet another major stage in our lives.

Bournemouth

I **should explain** that the appointment was not so much a proof of my abilities as the fact that the Children's Officer felt my inexperience would make me easier to handle and to mould me to her ways. I think she would have found the more experience applications too much of a challenge.

Bournemouth was one of the wealthy towns in England, a complete contrast to the rural villages of Wales. I had been introduced to the town in 1938, towards the end of my recuperation from the accident in the colliery – I was sent by the Miners' Welfare Association to a lovely hotel they had purchased opposite the Bournemouth pier. It had wonderful views over the sea, as well as easy access to the beautiful town. It was called the 'Court Royal', and was used for injured or sick coal miners to spend two weeks recuperating – free of charge.

Each morning at dawn, Council men would move across the beach, picking up every piece of litter and cigarette ends. The roads were swept every day; the parks in the town were always picturesque, with pools, flowerbeds, and squirrels everywhere. The shops were full of creature comforts and high-quality goods. I thoroughly enjoyed the 'high life' and returned to work shortly after that two weeks by the sea.

After this introduction to Bournemouth, I had no difficulty in persuading Sheila that this was the place to spend our honeymoon following our marriage during the Easter vacation. We had snow as well as sunshine but enjoyed our stay – exploring the surrounding countryside as well as the town.

These earlier visits helped us to settle fairly quickly into the favoured seaside resort. However, shortly after our arrival, Sheila's much admired and loved father was taken ill, and died suddenly. We were all shocked. Within days, her mother had sold the house in Cardiff and divided the proceeds between Sheila and her brother, Peter – on the assumption that for the rest of her days she could live with either the daughter or the son.

After the funeral, she returned with us to our rented flat and occupied the only bedroom – which meant that

Sheila and I had to climb a ladder over the staircase to sleep in the already overcrowded attic.

They were difficult days. Sheila found work in the local Tax Office, but my mother-in-law had no contacts in Bournemouth – and we were trying to adjust to our new jobs.

Soon we began the search for a house, which we found on the outskirts of Bournemouth, and moved in just before our first Christmas. It was the end house (detached), in a nice area, and served us all well for over thirty years.

Work

My work in the Children's Department proved both interesting and challenging. The Council had the care of about four hundred children under the age of sixteen. Two lady officers had charge of the girls, a nurse took care of the children under two, and I had the responsibility of caring for about ninety boys.

Bournemouth prided itself on having the highest proportion of 'children in care' placed in foster homes. There were two large residential homes for emergencies, but eighty-two percent of our children were in foster homes. We were a team of four to supervise these children and to visit them regularly (this included a periodic inspection of their sleeping arrangements). We interviewed the foster parents and children independently, and all our home visits had to be unannounced.

I had boys on a farm in Dorchester, thirty miles away, and also across the bay in Studland. The work thus involved much travelling, as well as report-writing, and making any necessary changes or adjustments that arose from time to time. Occasionally, I brought boys from the Juvenile Court when a magistrate had decided their homes were not good enough. Often, we had warning of such situations, and were able to make alternative arrangements.

We were lucky in having one very resourceful person whose home was always open for such unfortunate children. I don't remember any child who didn't benefit from her loving and accepting care.

Apart from the variety of family situations I had to deal with, I enjoyed travelling into the countryside when making the visits. I regarded myself as fortunate to have such a job, especially after my previous fourteen years in a coal mine.

Another development at this time was our decision to leave the Pentecostal movement and seek a more acceptable church where Sheila and I could worship happily. We discovered such in the East Cliff Congregational Church, where there was an inspiring preacher, a good choir, and a friendly congregation. We soon felt at home, became members, and involved ourselves in Sunday

School teaching.

Sheila sang in the choir, and I began taking services as a lay preacher in local and nearby rural churches. We delighted in our sense of being able to be Christians – yet free from denominational elements with which we had no sympathy or rapport. We were now proud to take any of our visitors to the church – including our parents. Although they did not agree with the theological and organisational differences, they were inspired by the fervent preaching and the warmth of the fellowship.

Whilst continuing my social work I soon resumed theological reading, and spent more and more time searching bookshops for inspiring books (especially by Harry Emerson Fosdick), and becoming more involved with the churches.

I also began a correspondence course with London University on New Testament Greek, and undertook studies towards a Bachelor of Divinity degree. My basic interests and the sense of 'Call' became increasingly more dominant, and I even considered training in the Congregational College at Bristol. I has an interview with the Principal, and was invited to become a student with a view to the full-time Ministry – but I could see no way in which I could maintain my commitments to mother-in-law and the house in Bournemouth. So, we continued with our respective jobs, whilst at the same time feeling the urge to continue preparation for work in and amongst the churches.

An Important Meeting

*A***nother dramatic break** came unexpectedly when our minister accepted an exchange of pulpits with an American minister from Chappaqua, New York. This was for three months. The American visitor was charming, and a good preacher. Some friends of our invited him and his wife to an evening in their home, and asked Sheila and me to join them. At first I protested I was too busy with work and studies, but John Smith replied, "Come on, you can give a few hours to these American visitors!" So we went.

During the evening John told Revd Nye about my work in the church and my interest in the Ministry. He listened with some curiosity. As we were about to leave, Revd Nye said, "D'you know, Ken, we have just the college for you in America, if you'll come over."

I made some light-hearted reply, to which he responded, "I'm serious about this – if you will be."

I said, "If that's the case, we'd better meet again and talk it over!"

On the way home Sheila said, "If you think I'm leaving Bournemouth to go to America, you've got another think coming!"

I replied, "Let's wait and see what happens."

What happened, was that Ken Nye contacted one of his elders who was also a Trustee of Bangor Theological Seminary in Maine, USA. He, in turn, contacted the seminary – as a result of which we received a telegram "Ken Roach accepted as a student for immediate commencement, come over in September." (This was the end of July, or early August).

Sheila and I thought and prayed deeply about the total situation, and then felt that this was an 'Open Door' into the Ministry. We decided to accept the invitation – in faith that here was another indication of the Divine Call.

The problems posed by the house, and mother-in-law, also resolved themselves miraculously. The Children's Department had taken in a homeless family of five children (all under twelve years) who had returned to England from South Africa. I had care of the boys, and had found them foster homes where the placements were working so well that the children began to feel as much affection for the foster parents as for their mother and father. The parents were becoming very concerned. Suddenly I thought, "Why not invite the family to occupy our house and, in return for a small rent, keep an eye on Sheila's mother?"

Needless to say, the family could hardly believe their good fortune. Mother-in-law accepted the arrangement (she occupied two rooms, while the family occupied the rest of the house), and we were able to move the family in just in time for the celebrations of Christmas 1956.

We arranged to sail on the *Queen Mary* on December 29th, and so another phase in our lives was concluded – only for us to embark on another in the USA.

Chapter 4

New York

*E*mbarking on the Cunard liner *Queen Mary* was to be another new experience. Neither Sheila nor I had previously been to sea. Unfortunately, we ran into the worst storm the liner had ever encountered!

Normally the ship docked in New York either dead on time or less than half an hour late. We eventually arrived a *day and a half* late. Day and night we plunged through mountainous waves – and a lot of crockery was lost, despite barriers erected around each table. Sleeping was as difficult, as was getting around the decks of this rolling 'mansion'.

The *Queen Mary* was a magnificent ship, every part being of the best quality design and construction (Fourteen years later we returned to England on the *QE2,* but felt that the ship was shoddy and utilitarian by comparison). The *Mary* was indeed the Queen of the seas, and we were privileged to have sailed in her – despite the storm.

On Friday January 4th, 1957 we arrived in New York. The sight of the skyscrapers on the horizon had excited our expectations and sailing past the Statue of Liberty was awesome. Friends from Chappaqua (a prosperous suburb of New York) were waiting, and soon we were on our way to their home – a journey of about thirty-five miles.

I have already referred to my discovery of the books of Harry Emerson Fosdick and his influence on my thought and religious development. Fosdick had gone through similar experiences himself. He was deeply committed to the Christian Faith but couldn't feel comfortable in the theological environment of his youth. He also felt the 'Call' to the Ministry but didn't know where this could be exercised. With only a vague faith, he embarked on a college training towards some form of minister. His autobiography spells out his predicament and faith:

> *"I headed for the ministry with very little that could presage a welcome by the Church. I was through the orthodox dogma. I had not the faintest interest in any sect or denomination.*

I could not have told clearly what I believed about any major Christian doctrine. I did not care. I wanted to make a contribution to the spiritual life of my generation. I said that to myself again and again. That was all I was sure about. If I prepared myself to make a spiritual contribution to my generation, somewhere a door would open; with that faith I headed toward the ministry."

(Fosdick, H.E., The Living of These Days – p57)

As we sailed into New York, this quote summed up my attitude very well. We had transferred to a Congregational Church in Bournemouth, and had been sponsored by a Congregational minister in America. (Congregationalism is related to Unitarianism, and features a broad, inclusive theology). I was clear as to the fundamentalist theology I was leaving behind, but not certain as to my theological position in the future.

I simply felt strongly that my life's vocation was to be in some form of Christian ministry and that a door would open which we would regard as divine guidance. Sheila and I felt this so deeply that we had 'burned our boats' in the UK and sailed in faith to this new land.

Fosdick's guiding star was a determination to look into the human situation, and then ask what the Christian

Faith had to say about it. Most of his sermons would open with a depiction of a human predicament:

"How can we believe in a good God in a world like this?"

"How can I understand the Bible?"

"Where can I find a Faith for tough times?"

"What does it mean to be a real person?"

"What does the divinity of Jesus really mean?"

"Can I believe in immorality?"

Fosdick wrote more than twenty books. Most of them are collections of twenty-five sermons – all were motivated by intelligent questions facing honest people and each of them deals with the questions clearly and with practical realism. Readers have found them stimulating and most satisfying.

Fosdick also developed a wide listenership to his radio broadcasts, and was responsible for many men and women deciding to go into the Ministry. Under his inspiration, aspiring ministers and honest Christians felt they could be open to all their doubts, yet be rich in faith and spirituality.

With all this input from Fosdick, and knowing he was still alive, I had often thought how thrilled I would be if I could only see him from a distance. Imagine my response when, during our first meal at his home, Revd

Ken Nye rather casually asked, "How would you like to meet Fosdick?"

I looked at him in silence.

He continued, "I wrote to Fosdick and told him of his influence over you and your coming here for training for the ministry; would he meet you? To which Fosdick had replied, 'Bring him down!'."

So, on a snowy Monday morning January 7th, my sponsor took me to Fosdick's home in the Bronx where, on arrival, the great man opened the door, came to greet me in the front garden, took my coat, and led us into his living room and library. On the way, I asked Ken Nye what was the secret of Fosdick's life. He replied, "Fosdick took his work very seriously – and himself very lightly. For every minute he was in the pulpit, an hour of preparation had been spent in the study."

I don't remember much of the conversation that morning, for I was overawed and tongue-tied; but I did relate an occasion when I had told a visiting Apostolic pastor that I was reading Fosdick – to which the response (with bitterness) had been, "Fosdick? Fosdick! The greatest rotter that ever wrote a book!" At which Harry Emerson threw back his head with a hearty laugh and said, "Kenneth, I've been called worse things than that!"

From the library, Fosdick gave me a copy of his autobiography, duly inscribed with cordial goodwill, plus his latest book of sermons, "What is vital in religion?"

Months later, one of the lecturers in the Seminary told me he had attended a conference where Fosdick was present – and he had asked after my progress. Such was Fosdick – the man, as well as the preacher. Endlessly interested in people, their problems and, especially, how he could help aspiring ministers. He always had a leisurely attitude, an attentive ear, and an understanding heart for everyone. Although he made many bitter enemies among Fundamentalists and was thrown out of the Presbyterian Church because of his theology, he understood their difficulties – and was sympathetic rather than vindictive.

Fosdick was a great Christian. Eventually, a wealthy friend, John D Rockefeller, built him one of the finest churches in New York – the Riverside Church. Here membership was inclusive of all Faiths and every variety of Christian beliefs. It was a magnificent building of twenty storeys – open seven days a week and twenty-four hours a day for anyone in need of physical, psychological or spiritual help.

We worshipped there on January 13th. The preacher was Dr McCracken, who had succeeded Fosdick to the pulpit there. His text was from the Old Testament - the story of the three Hebrew lads thrown into a furnace for their faith, only for the onlookers to see a fourth person with them "like the Son of Man."

Sheila and I found great assurance in the sermon; we knew we were 'three' having gone to New York, and the third was "like the Son of Man." Whether I have lived up to all this idealism and these privileges is for others to say, but I am eternally grateful to Harry Emerson Fosdick and his willingness to give me a morning in his home to begin my first week in America.

Fosdick had a very socially active wife; she was out speaking to a group when I visited. They had two daughters who had been given every opportunity to live full, active lives – including at least a year studying in Europe.

Without knowing all the facts, we often tend to think of such families as ideal; not having to cope with some of the problems of lesser mortals. One daughter had climbed the social ladder and was working among top American politicians; she was known internationally for her contributions.

Imagine my shock a few years ago to see her name and picture on one of the obituary pages of *The Guardian* newspaper – Dorothy Fosdick had died. There were two columns outlining her outstanding contributions in her field of work, but, sadly, also a paragraph telling of her intimate involvement with a senior American politician who could have become President of the USA. Dorothy had been devastated to learn that he was a two-timer, and had been sleeping with another woman whilst in an intimate relationship with herself.

My thoughts of sympathy went from Dorothy to her parents. After giving so much of their lives to higher idealism for themselves and their family, Dorothy's treatment must have been a painful experience. For a family with so much in the public eye, with a daughter equally successful in other ways, the discovery of such a betrayal in the sight of the world mush have been a crushing blow to them all.

I'm sure Fosdick's faith carried him through, and he may have felt some consolation in the whole world knowing that big trouble can find its way into the hearts of the best families.

None of us is exempt from heartbreak, however near to God we may have lived and worked. Such experiences bring the 'highest' into a common cause with the 'lowest' showing that, in the last resort, each of us is part of the basic human family – with all its high-peak experiences and low-depth devastations. I can only hope that, in their day of profound need for consolation and comfort, the Fosdick's found support from at least some of those to whom they had given so much.

Maine

*W*e **stayed** in Chappaqua for about three weeks. On the first Sunday we were attending the service at the Congregational Church when the Minister made an announcement. "The Roaches are here from England with just seven suitcases of possessions. They will soon be going to Maine, where an empty apartment will be found for them. Anyone with a spare bed, carpet, or piece of furniture – please bring it to Ed Thompson's barn as soon as possible!"

The result was yet another miracle. Everything we needed was given (no duplicates, except two beds); they even provided a typewriter and filing cabinet. In due course the gifts were sent to Maine on a truck, and were duly installed in our student apartment by the time we arrived.

Sheila and I were put on a plane – this was our first-ever flight – and sent on our way. We won't forget the journey. It was a small plane. Soon we sensed some unease. An announcement was made that something was wrong with an engine – and we were going to turn back. About fifteen minutes later came another announcement, "The engine seems to have righted itself, and we shall resume our flight."

This was hardly the best introduction to flying, but we did arrive in Maine. There we were met by representatives of the Seminary, who took us to our destination by car.

Maine is one of the most northerly States in the US (it borders Canada). It is the fourth poorest State in the country. The Seminary, the second oldest training institution for Congregational ministers, is situated in Bangor city.

This position was ideal in many ways. Most of the students were of mature age; some had large families. Most had experiences in various occupations, as well as in church life, and were able to undertake the care of a rural church that had a manse (where they could be housed as the student minister's family).

In Maine, the churches couldn't afford full-time ministers, so the Seminary was a good source of such services. The churches helped to solve many of the problems presented by students needing some income, pastoral experiences, and accommodation for their families. It worked well, to the mutual advantage of all concerned.

Despite the Seminary being ideal for mature students, it did not in any way compromise its academic standards. Every student was expected to learn Greek, or Hebrew, so they could read the Old or New Testament in the original language. The staff were amongst the best in their field, and the national recognition for their writings.

The January Convocation featured lectures by international theologians, and gave the students a chance over four days to hear and to question well-known people. One of the first I heard was Paul Tillich, a thinker respected worldwide. Another, one of the Niebuhr brothers, was also of international repute.

The Convocation took place between two semesters (terms) and provided a good opportunity for staff and students to rest and recuperate from the first term of studies, before embarking on the second.

The subject at the Seminary were traditional for such an institution; theology (ancient and modern), Old and New Testament in breadth and depth, Church history, and pastoral psychology. There was also a Professor for practical ministry who gave regular lectures on pastoral problems, as well as supervising student preaching and placements. He visited the churches where students had been placed, and so was able to discuss problems from the perspective of the church as well as that of the prospective pastor.

It was a well-balanced curriculum, and there was also the interaction of the student as they shared their background experiences as well as their reaction to the Seminary training. We often met in a student apartment on a Friday evening to relax, and to talk things over from the student's point of view.

The week began on Monday afternoon, when students from pastoral placements returned in time for the 'preaching practice' in the Seminary church. On such occasions a student would construct the full service – while the others listed critically as well as sympathetically. Then, before leaving, each listener would complete a questionnaire about the choice of hymns, shape of the prayers, length and quality of the sermon, and general pulpit deportment. It was all very constructive. Later, the leader of worship would have a long session with the Professor on every aspect of the performance (including the other students' comments!). Student pastors in parishes would also have to consider the views and evaluations of their congregations, as well as the opinions of their parishioners.

For the first year I did some preaching in various

churches for which, of course, I needed transport. Neither Sheila nor I had ever driven a car, but we soon realised we would have to add this to the necessary skills. Sheila had been given work in the Bangor Public Library, so some money was being earned. A very practically minded student friend took us to a second-hand car dealer, selected a 'Plymouth' model, negotiated a big reduction in the price, and then drove us back to our apartment.

This was yet another new set of experiences and skills to acquire. Another student friend and his wife undertook to give me lessons and, eventually, I was driving on the 'right' side of the road with reasonable confidence.

Student Pastor

*T*owards the end of the year I was introduced to a student pastorate abut ninety miles north, close to the Canadian border. Sherman Mills was a rural community, almost entirely given over to potato crowing. There was only one church there, and nearly all the town folk were Protestants. The church was the centre of the village in every way – for all the age groups.

My first preaching assignment there was on a November Sunday. We woke early to prepare for the long drive, as well as the conducting of worship. It was a cold morning. The roads were icy, and as soon as we entered the road from the Seminary our car spun around out of control. We had already learned that Americans are used to such conditions and always regard them as challenges to be confronted. We were also keen to see our assignment for the day, which could possibly lead to a student pastorate. We righted the car, and proceeded very cautiously for the ninety-mile journey, through several uninhabited areas. With great care, we finally arrived at the top of the hill – below which was Sherman Mills.

I decided to put the car into second gear, so as not to depend entirely on the brakes. No sooner had I released the clutch … the car turned around out of control, moved backwards towards the side of the road, drifted slowly down a bank, and came to rest against a tree about twenty yards off the road! It was now about ten o'clock; the service started at ten thirty. We pulled ourselves out of the car, climbed the bank, and slithered down the hill – arriving at the church at ten twenty-nine. We were gratefully received but expected to carry on with the service – which I did!

Having completed the service of worship, I told some elders of my plight and our concerns for the car. Their response was to place a textbook in my hand and say, "OK. You teach the senior high Sunday School Class, and we'll fetch your car!"

I couldn't believe what I was hearing (but soon realised I was probably the best person to teach a religious lesson, and they were much better able to retrieve the car). Imagine our relief when, after the full morning session in the church, we found the car sitting outside waiting for us!

After being taken for a meal we drove back to the Seminary, probably speechless most of the way – but nevertheless full of wonderment at what had happened, and with admiration for the people who seemed to be able to take all those things in their stride. Apparently the three Mitchell brothers, who were responsible for keeping the roads open, had seen my car when sweeping the road. They rescued it from the tree, and left it on the side of the road where the elders found it – and brought it to the church!

After more 'preaching with a view' occasions, and mutual discussions, I was invited to be the student pastor at Sherman Mills.

With brother Hayden *(right)* in the early days

My parents Alice and Ernest

Our wedding day

Our first home in Bournemouth

Seeing the year out in style – our voyage to New York aboard the Queen Mary

Sherman Mills in 1960. My student pastorate was at the church – Washburn Memorial Church

From coalpit to pulpit – delivering a sermon at Washburn Memorial Church. The church had beautiful windows

Sunday School at Sherman Mills. Sheila is at the front on the left

REV. KENNETH ROACH

Sherman Mills Church Receives New Minister

SHERMAN MILLS, Feb. 4—The Rev. Kenneth E. Roach has assumed the pastorate of the Washburn Memorial Congregational church at Sherman Mills. Mr. and Mrs. Roach are residing at the parsonage on the weekends and in Bangor during the week where Mr. Roach is a student pastor at the Bangor Theological Seminary.

The Rev. Roach, 36, was born in the village of Kenfig Hill, South Wales. He worked for thirteen years as a Welsh coal miner where he obtained a miner's scholarship at the University of Swansea in South Wales where he received his Social Science degree. He took a post in Bournemouth, England as a Children's Welfare office in charge of ninety boys in foster homes. He was a laymen for 17 years in various country churches.

In the summer of 1956 in an exchange of pastorates between an English church and a New York church, the visiting minister learned of Mr. Roach's desire to enter the ministry. Through the efforts of this minister and other people Mr. Roach was able to come to America in January, 1957 and enroll at the Bangor Theological Seminary. After arrival in Bangor, he worked for the Family Service Society for the summer and part time after becoming a student pastor.

He is married to the former Shelia Myfanwy Bishop of Wales. Mrs. Roach is employed at the Bangor Public Library.

Rev. K. E. Roach Ordained At Sherman Rite

SHERMAN, July 28—The Rev. Kenneth E. Roach, of Bournemouth, England, was ordained to the Christian ministry Sunday afternoon at the Washburn Memorial Congregational Church in Sherman Mills.

The Ecclesiastical Council of the Aroostook Association examined the credentials of the pastor. The examination was followed by the acceptance of the council to ordain the candidate in accordance with the request of the church which was read by Mrs. Floyd Martin, church clerk. The Rev. Francis E. Hawes was elected moderator. The Rev. John Morrison was scribe.

The service of ordination began with an organ prelude by Mrs. Robert Somers. The call to worship and invocation was given by the Rev. John Morrison, pastor of the Congregational Church at Ashland, and the scripture was read by Monroe Palmer, student pastor of the Whittier Congregational Church at Island Falls.

The ordination sermon was preached by Dr. Burton Throckmorton, professor of the New Testament at the Bangor Theological Seminary. The address to the ordained was given by the Rev. Francis E. Hawes, pastor of the East Millinocket Congregational Church. The laying on of hands, by the ministers present, was followed by the ordination prayer by the Rev. Kenneth E. Nye, minister of the First Congregational Church at Choppaqua, N. Y.

The congregation participated in the hymn singing and the choir sang the anthem, directed by Mrs. Harry James. The organ accompaniment was by Mrs. Robert Somers.

A buffet supper was served following the service. Deaconesses Mrs. Thomas Splan, Mrs. Beverly Rand, Mrs. Jackman Sleeper, assisted by Mrs. George Evans, were in charge of the supper.

Flowers were donated by Mrs. Philip Trafton and Mrs. Daniel Curtis and arranged by Mrs. Clifton Bragden.

Mr. and Mrs. Roach will vacation in England during the month of August. They plan to go by plane from Boston Tuesday evening. Upon their arrival in England, they will visit their families and friends in Bournemouth and Wales. Mr. Roach will conduct services at the East Cliff Congregational Church at Bournemouth August 28. They plan to return to America by the first of September.

The pastor will deliver his last sermon here at the Washburn Memorial Congregational Church September 4. Mr. and Mrs. Roach will leave for Utica, N. Y. September 6 where he has accepted a pastorate in the Bethesda Congregational Church and he will assume his new duties there September 11.

Assessing the fallen tree by our garage with Sheila's mum, Edith – my wielding of the axe impressed the locals

Graduation day with Sheila at Bangor Theological Seminary

Farewell Party At Sherman For Rev. Kenneth E. Roach

Rev. and Mrs. Kenneth E. Roach

Sherman Mills — Parishioners of the Washburn Memorial Congregational Church at Sherman Mills, honored their pastor and his wife at a surprise farewell party recently. Rev. and Mrs. Kenneth E. Roach have gone to Utica, N. Y., where he has assumed the pastorate at the Bethesda Congregational Church.

The party climaxed a slide lecture which the Roachets gave on their native country, Wales and southern England. They also showed scenes of Scotland and Ireland. They spent their vacation there in August.

A purse of money was presented to Mr. and Mrs. Roach by the senior deacon Thomas Splan. Refreshments were served from a table of red and white color scheme. The couple cut the first slice of a decorated cake made for them by Mrs. Clifton Bragdon. Mrs. Herbert Perrin supplied the table appointments.

Mr. Roach has been pastor at Sherman Mills for the past three years. The Washburn Memorial Church was his first parish in America. In June of this year he was graduated from the Bangor Theological Seminary with a Batchelor of Divinity Degree. He received his Social Science Degree at the University of Swansea, South Wales. Welfare work has also been among his training.

Installation Is Tomorrow

The Rev. Kenneth E. Roach, a native of Kenfig Hill, South Wales, will be installed as pastor of the Bethesda Welsh Congregationalist Church, at 7:30 tomorrow night.

Participating in the installation service will be: the Rev. Harold R. Fray, moderator of the Oneida Assn. and pastor of Plymouth Congregational Church; the Rev. Rees T. Williams, Oswego, and former pastor of Bethesda; the Rev. Bruce Roberts, executive secretary of the Council of Churches in Syracuse and Onondaga County; the Rev. M. Jack Takayanagi, pastor of South Congregational Church; Dr. R. Glynne Lloyd, pastor of Moriah Presbyterian Church; the Rev. Harold McGilvray, chairman of the Credentials Committee for the Oneida Assn. and the Rev. Kenneth E. Nye, who will give the sermon.

Evan M. Evans, senior deacon, will also take part.

REV. K. E. ROACH

NEW PASTOR GREETED—The Rev. Kenneth Roach, second from left, new pastor of Bethesda Congregationalist Church, was greeted by area ministers last night. From the left, The Rev. Harold R. Fray, Plymouth Congregationalist Church, who served as moderator; Mr. Roach; The Rev. Rees T. Williams, former pastor at Bethesda, and the Rev. Kenneth E. Nye, of Chappaqua, who gave the sermon.

Plymouth-Bethesda United Reformed Church, Utica, New York; and our Manse on Dickinson Street

Collecting the first of our adopted daughters in February 1964 *(above)*. Alison *(below)*

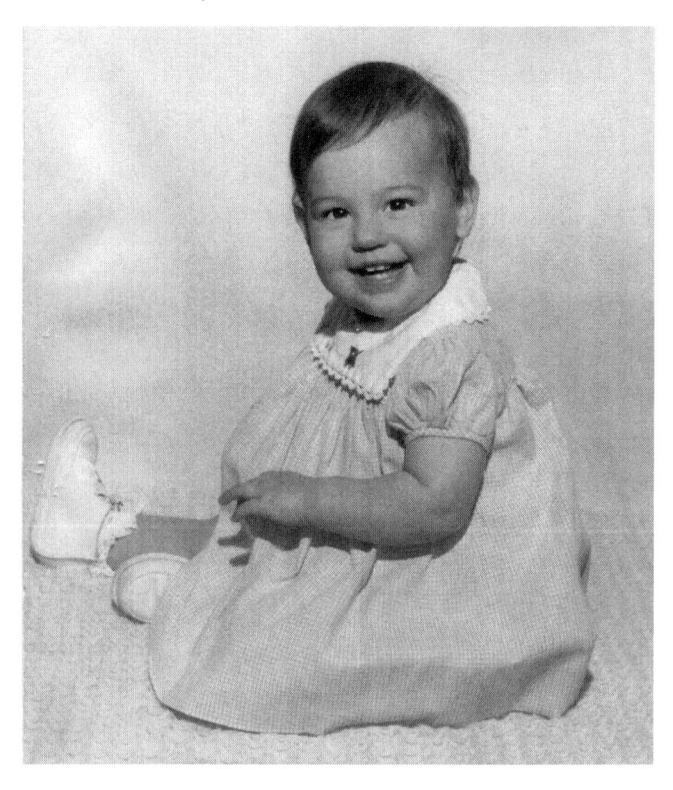

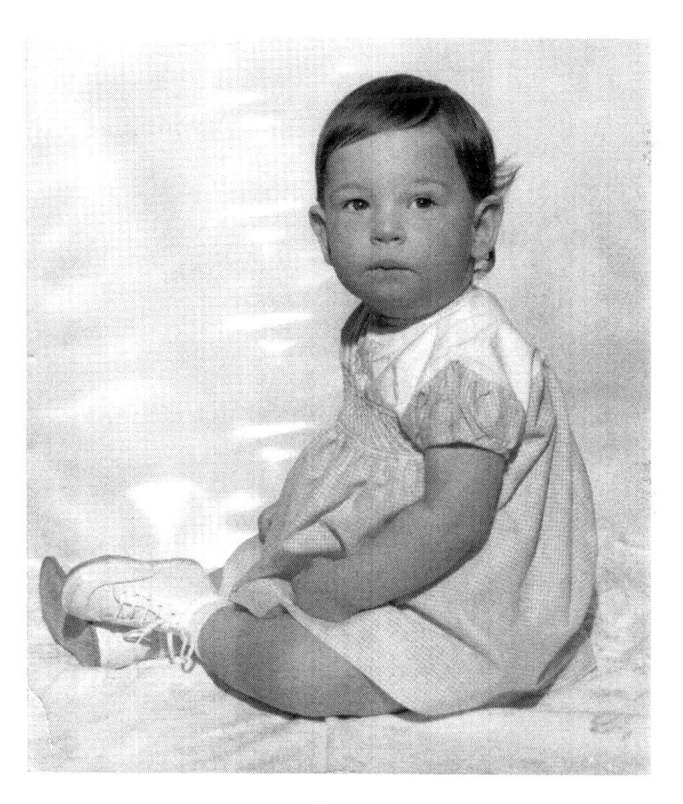

Hilary

The whole family enjoyed our summer retreats at
Trenton Assembly Park

With Sheila, Alison and Hilary

250 Attend Welsh Event

The annual St. David's Day banquet at the Hotel Utica last night was attended by more than 250 people of Welsh descent.

Guest soloist at the dinner honoring the Welsh's patron saint was R. Wayne Walters, a frequent winner in Eisteddfod and other Welsh song competitions.

The Rev. Hedd-Wynn Williams, minister of St. Paul's United Church of Scarborough, Ontario, Canada, spoke on "Welsh Characters I Have Known."

The setting for his talk was a mining village in Wales. Mr. Williams told guests that their ancestors had left them a heritage rich in devotion to the church, to themselves and the arts.

Sponsoring last night's observance were the Goronwy Lodge No. 37 and Gwenfron Lodge No. 5, Order of American True Ivorites.

The Rev. Kenneth E. Roach, pastor of Bethesda Congregational Church, was toastmaster. The invocation was given by the Rev. John Meirion Lloyd, moderator of the General Assembly of Presbyterians in Assam, India.

THEY TALKED AND SANG . . . Utica's Welsh people observed St. David's Day at a banquet held in Hotel Utica last night. Mrs. Katherine Hughes talked with the Rev. Hedd-Wynn M. Williams (center), and Rev. Kenneth E. Roach, toastmaster, before the dinner.

Our best friends in Utica, Jack and Marie – Mr and Mrs D.

Back to England: Pastor at Castle Green Congregational Church in Bristol

Right: In the pulpit at Castle Green Congregational Church in Bristol

Below: Enjoying retirement with Hayden *(left)* and Sheila

With Sheila at home in 2017. We were able to buy our manse in Castle Green after I retired

Surounded by books and music

Chapter 5

Between Two Homes

Our invitation to the student parish at Sherman Mills inevitably meant that some changes had to be made to our lifestyle at Bangor Theological College. We divided our furniture, so we were able to sleep at the Parsonage in Sherman Mills at the weekends whilst, for the next six months, we also occupied a student flat at Bangor. Sheila and I commuted to the parish on Friday afternoons, and returned on Mondays. Probably half the students were doing much the same. When the summer break came, we moved to Sherman. Sheila lived there alone during term-time for the remaining two years, whilst I attended classes at the Seminary.

The studies represented a good, broad training in preparation for the Christian Ministry. Biblical studies were the base, but modern theology and sociology were also part of the curriculum. The students came from a wide variety of backgrounds, so the discussions were interesting. I well remember one student voicing a Conservative bias, challenging the Professor of Philosophy on his Liberal views to which came the calm, measured reply, "I'm glad I wasn't brought up in a Christian home; I haven't had as much to 'unlearn' as some people."

My basic quest was to try to understand more clearly and realistically what 'Salvation' means to human experience. In my younger days, I had been drilled in the necessity of being 'saved' – so as to avoid hell and go to heaven. I had accepted that once 'saved' you were a citizen of the Kingdom of God, enjoying the Light, whilst the unsaved lived in darkness.

Having rejected the exclusiveness of such theology I felt there was a basic Reality, to be discovered for myself, that needed to be interpreted in order to minister more effectively to others. For years I had been moving in this direction, and I wanted the Seminary training to help me to continue to progress towards a fuller understanding.

It was relatively easy to keep the machinery of the churches going – with their celebrations, social activities, hymn singing worship services, and the appropriate ministrations at births, marriages, and deaths. However, I needed a firmer place on which to stand theologically.

This 'vision of faith' needed to relate to the ever-deepening insights of psychology as it struggled with the concerns of mental health and mature relationships.

Fosdick had also done much work in this field. Most of his sermons tried to deal with profoundly personal problems. One of his books carries the title, "On Being a Real Person." Here he deals with such problems as how to handle the excessive guilt of a mischievous conscience, as well as how to find adequate resources in the inner world to deal with difficulties confronted in the outer world.

Most of the lecturers dealt with more objective material, but when it came to writing essays I almost always used a variation of my main concern; salvation. So I would write, for example, on the concept of salvation in Luke's gospel – or in the early Church. Eventually, when having to submit a thesis for the Divinity degree, I took the title, "The Concept of Salvation in the Parables of Jesus."

Whilst I feel there are no final, definitive answers to any of the profound questions of life, I did find a firmer foundation on which to build an affirmative, yet ever-creative, preaching ministry. The main difference between a Fundamentalist and a Liberal is that the former affirms there are black and white answers that must be believed in order to gain salvation. By contrast, a Liberal has some basics of faith that he feels can be trusted; life is regarded as a constant journey of re-definition and re-adjustment to new insights and ever-challenging new experiences.

Fundamentalism makes a strong appearance in uncertain and dangerous times, when people feel they need something positive and picturesque to sustain them. This is perfectly understandable, and requires sympathy and support. Many ordinary folk have overwhelming problems in life – and need all the help they can get, from whatever source. In most cases they probably do not have the necessary education or emotional strength to consider all the options in developing a concept of Truth, nor a faith that can change when change is indicated (without feeling threatened existentially).

"The Place on which to Stand" is not a series of credal statements, nor a final theological conclusion to be defended at all costs. It is more of an indefinable state in the heart, a conviction that there is eternal truth, though our finite minds will never comprehend it. In that, we can know God in 'gnosis', though we will never know anything about Him in 'pistis' (two Greek words for 'knowledge').

With this basic faith, we can "Rest in the Lord" while at the same time continue to change, grow and mature in faith and honest relationships. I believe this was the fruit of my theological studies that became the guiding principle of my continuing ministry.

It is still the stance of my present life-style, which some may think too introspective (I must confess to having some misgivings myself). However, some Biblical insights do suggest – for example "Keep the heart with all diligence, for out of it are the issues of life" (Prov.4.23); and the teaching of Jesus, "In patience preserve your soul."

Certainly, we live in a world where we are super-skilled in the construction of things, a world filled with consumerism and buildings. We are, however, in danger of losing our personal values, thereby distorting our relationships and indulging the selfish clamour of our ego-selves.

Despite the strangeness of its language, personal salvation and a sense of oneness in community are basic necessities of human beings in every age. To this endless concern; I have tried to direct my preaching ministry and pastoral activities.

Travelling across Maine

*A*n **interesting** and beneficial feature of the Seminary years was that the Professor of Philosophy took a special interest in the welfare of Sheila and myself. He (Bradshaw) was much admired for his tall, handsome physique and cultured mind, but was not particularly popular with students of staff. For several years, a movement to merge four denominations (each being of the Congregational type) had been in progress. Bradshaw was against the idea, and wrote a book expressing his opposition to the proposed merger in the strongest terms. He stood head and shoulders in every way above the rest of the staff, including the President, and this rather isolated him. His calm demolition of student challenges has already been mentioned, and the fact that he was the only person on the staff who drove a Cadillac car also set him apart!

In this impressive vehicle, Marion John Bradshaw travelled all over the State of Maine, taking numerous pictures of the beautiful countryside. He had published four books extolling the State, and used a favourite (mis) quote from the New Testament; "I have learned to be content in whatever state I am – as long as it is the State of Maine!"

Sheila and I were invited to join him on some of these trips – and we were often part of his search to find new photographs, and the best perspective. The Cadillac carried his large tripod, stretched from corner to corner, of the company of which we had to accommodate ourselves! Bradshaw always accepted our invitation to have tea with us, and I think he was pleased to be entertaining "these visitors from England."

An unforgettably special occasion was when he invited us to spend a week with him at a Unitarian Conference on an island ten miles off the New England coast. Star Island was small, but beautiful, and featured a conference centre and a stone church on its most elevated position. One could walk around the coast in a matter of a few hours. There were no houses or electricity, and worshippers at the evening prayers each had to take a candle for light. The light in the church, therefore, was in direct proportion to the number or worshippers. It was an inspiring sight, after supper, to see a line of these lit candles making their way up the hill for final meditations.

Discussions and lecturers were of the liberal approach to religious questions, and under the leadership of prominent theologians and academic figures. Some of the visiting lecturers were selected to be deliberately provocative. I remember one atheistic biologist saying to a group at a lunch table, after a delicious lobster meal, "Of course you know what all you people really are, don't you? Just lumps of digested vegetables!"

Our friend paid all expenses, thereby giving us a most memorable and stimulating holiday. Our thoughts were challenged. Nevertheless, the purpose of the centre was to help people to find positive convictions – in spite of questioning all the orthodox theological creeds.

The Professor was basically devout, as well as being the most sceptical member of staff. He usually walked into the classroom right on time to begin the lecture, and simply stood behind the desk without saying a word. The class became quiet. Bradshaw put his hands on the desk, bowed his head, and always prayed the same prayer:

O God,
For the enrichment of our lives and the advancement of Thy Kingdom,
grant us the insights of Truth,
the inspiration of Love,
and the guidance of your Spirit,
Amen.

I think Bradshaw composed it himself; it certainly reflected his thought – and was a source of inspiration (though everyone did not regard him as loveable!).

Sherman Mills

*O***n moving** into the Parsonage at Sherman Mills in June 1958, Sheila and I began another stage of learning about American life and our ministry there. Sheila became very involved, attending the women's groups almost nightly. She made close friendships which lasted years. She sand in the choir and provided most of the leadership of two active youth groups. During term-times, from Monday to Friday, she lived alone in the huge, detached house – whilst I had a room in the Seminary.

For a woman of only twenty-eight years, this required courage and resourcefulness – which she showed plenty. She needed these because, as with all rural communities, Sherman had its violent past – as well as occasional house visits from the wildlife!

Early in our ministry we were told of a former town clerk who had been murdered, and that the man who killed him was about to be released from prison. Apparently, he was a simple, trusting farmer who had paid his annual council rent in cash, but hadn't asked for a receipt. Later, the clerk denied he had been paid, and demanded the rent again. The farmer couldn't prove the transaction, and perhaps doubted his memory – so paid his rent the second time.

Not satisfied with one deceit, the clerk tried his trick once more. At this, the former realised he was being cheated, went home, collected his gun, returned, and shot the clerk as he sat at his desk. The farmer, having served his sentence in prison, returned to the neighbourhood whilst we were there. He settled in a remote wooden hut, and most people didn't see him again.

One Sunday morning, Sheila was aware of whispers among the choir members and overheard the remark, "I think he pushed her in."

Asking for clarification, she was told of a lady on the outskirts of the village who used to enjoy watching the fish in their garden pond. She would lie on the edge, with goggles over her eyes. The report was that she had been found dead at the bottom of the pond, subsequently I conducted the funeral. I remember that there was no enquiry into the 'accident', or any presence of police or sheriffs. Mr 'S'. was acting strangely, and people were very suspicious.

On the evening of the funeral, I was attending a meeting in the church. Sheila was at home, alone, when there came a knock at the door. The widower asked to see me. Rather nervously, Sheila invited him in and commiserated on the loss of his wife saying he must have had a very sad day.

"Oh no, not at all," came the reply, rather cheerfully, "I've had lots of company, the best food I've had in a long time, and I simply want to pay the Reverend for a lovely service."

After such a conversation with my apprehensive wife, he handed her a ten-dollar note for my services – and left.

Another dramatic occasion was when a teenager murdered his stepfather. The family lived on the outskirts of the village, and the husband was known for abusing his wife. The boy had warned him that if it continued, he would shoot him. The school bus had brought the boy home one day to find another beating taking place in the garden.

Without being noticed – the boy went into the house, loaded the family shotgun, and joined the rowing couple. On seeing her son, the mother realised what was about to happen and tried to shield her husband with her left arm. The boy fired a multiple-type shot. The pellets riddled the man's body, and injured his mother's left arm and shoulder. I saw the undertaker's van race through the village at a dangerous speed towards the hospital in the next village, and knew something serious had happened. The story was soon common knowledge; the man dead on arrival.

The fourteen year-old was arrested and taken to Bangor Prison. The general feeling amongst the adults and youth was of sympathy for the lad, who had come to the end of his tether. About six weeks later, I received a phone call from the Probation Officer in Bangor. He was concerned for the boy, whose trial was to be held in a week or so. Would I, as a community minister, speak to as many people as possible to ascertain the general feeling – and speak accordingly at the trial?

I agreed to do this and found that almost everyone was sorry for the lad. They were sure he was not basically violent and was a victim rather than a culprit. They said they'd be glad to have him back in the village and would do all they could to help him rebuild his family life again. There was only one objector I can recall, unfortunately one of my deaconesses who rather self-righteously said, "He murdered his stepfather and should receive his punishment."

I attended the trial, and was the last witness to be called. I can still see the judge – after my presentation on behalf of the community – shrouded in a large black cloak, head slightly bowed, and tapping a pen on a notepad. He remained in this posture of deep thought for some minutes. The courtroom was frozen with anticipation. They boy stood pale, and expressionless. Over fifty years later I can still remember the judge's exact words.

He slowly raised his head and said, "Well, 'D'. I'm going to listen to your Pastor and let you go home, on two years' probation." There was a huge sigh of relief. I returned home to Sherman Mills, with mother and son in my car. They were not members of my church but, on leaving the car, they said "You'll see us in church on Sunday!" This was Friday afternoon.

Sunday morning came. The service had stared, and the church was fairly full. During the responsive reading of a Psalm, the door opened and a woman entered with a white pillow under her left arm – swathed in bandages. A boy followed, and they had to sit just in front of the pulpit. The atmosphere was electric. I preached on the importance of second (and more than one) chance to make good.

The text was a scene from the book of Acts – in which John Mark felt he couldn't continue with the mission of Paul and Barnabas and subsequently left them to return home. Paul felt this was a betrayal. When a second mission was being planned, Barnabas suggested that he and Paul should give Mark another chance, and include him again. Paul refused to allow this, and the contention between them became so sharp that Paul and Barnabas went their separate ways, and Silas accompanied Paul.

Scholars are convinced that the same John Mark wrote the earliest Gospel (from which Matthew and Luke quoted heavily). In other words; if Barnabas had not given Mark a second chance, and trusted him, we may have been deprived of the first three Gospels.

Life in rural Maine was insecure in many ways. Each autumn, men went into the woods to hunt deer. Sometimes, the compass they always carried went 'sour'. Some men simply disappeared for good. One such story, fortunately, had a very happy ending. The local grocer left home one Saturday morning to hunt, saying he'd be back by 3.00.pm to help his wife finish the day's business. Bill went into the local woods, hunted for a while, decided it was time to eat his lunch, and then to return home. He sat on the trunk of a fallen tree and, at about 2.00.pm, headed (as he thought) for home out of the dense woods. He walked for some time but then, to his horror, found himself back where he'd eaten his lunch! His compass had failed.

As happens with people in such a situation, he thought he'd been walking in a straight line).

We will now divert in the story and return to folk in the village. At 3.00.pm, concern for Bill was being mentioned in his store; by 3.30.pm, fears were being expressed that yet another hunter had been lost in the trackless forest. Three men were sitting, smoking and chatting, outside the Post Office, when one of them had a bright idea. "Let's go into the church," he said; and off they went.

Meanwhile, Bill was thinking of all the implications of his possible death. Suddenly, he heard a familiar sound coming from the distance. He recognised the church bells, and realised they could give him the direction home. He left his gun behind; and hurried towards the familiar sound. He thought he'd only have minutes to benefit from the bells, for he knew no reason for their ringing. It was a Saturday afternoon, so there could be no funeral or special service, and he'd heard of no wedding having been arranged.

He lunged forward through the undergrowth as fast as he could, making a straight line towards the 'music'. The ringing continued, and eventually Bill realised the bells were probably being rung to try to guide him out of the woods. With profound gratitude and tears of deep joy he relaxed – but still walked very purposefully. Finally, he emerged on the road that would re-unite him with his very relieved family. The community had also found a new appreciation for their church bells – their ability to stop at least one man going around in circles and guiding him out of the trackless wood!

Sherman Mills, from 1958-1960, provided us with the endless series of new experiences and challenges. In the next village, Island Fells, we discovered a Scottish couple where the man was the minister of the Congregational Church. We became friends, and shared some ministries as well as social occasions.

We were not far from the Canadian border at Houlton where, out of curiosity, we drove one evening. We found the border, over which were the look-out posts above the road. We were speculating as to whether they were Canadian or American. With a sense of fun, we astonished the border guards by standing in the middle of the road, singing "God Save the Queen"!

Wildlife was plentiful – bears, deer, skunk and moose, as well as smaller animals. The road called 'Nine Miles Woods' approaching Sherman Mills could be interesting to drive through in the dark. Along both sides of the road there would be hundreds of pairs of shining eyes, and we knew that at any time animals might wander onto the highway. A confrontation with a big moose could damage a car, so extra care was essential. The road referred to was nine miles long, without a house or dwelling of any kind and, if one was alone, the possibility of a 'night out' was not exactly attractive, especially on a winter's night – when the temperature might be well below zero Fahrenheit.

Most of the villages were 12-15 miles away; the next town was about forty. Sherman Mills was an entirely Protestant community whereas Benedicta, just five miles away, was wholly Roman Catholic. I remember no effective co-operation between these two communities. This was long before the Ecumenical movement of the mid-sixties but, in any case, our work in Sherman and my studies kept us both fully occupied.

Sherman Mills, built in a hollow, was quite picturesque. The centre was triangular, each side being bout two hundred yards long. The lower section contained the recreation park, on which stood a bandstand. Moving up the natural slope, the church occupied the top corner – whilst along a level road towards the east was the Manse (or the 'Parsonage'). This had a huge barn attached; beside it, towards the church, was a small building which had once been a public library.

The church doors were never locked, and anyone could go in at any time for quiet meditation. Behind the pulpit was a full-length stained-glass window in rich colours , depicting Jesus with outstretched arms and a soft, welcoming face. It was a superb, beautiful picture, providing constant inspiration as well as being a continuing reminder of what the church is all about. The kitchen was well equipped for meals and social occasions, with plenty of space for communal activities.

Music for worship was provided by a piano, which I soon considered inadequate. On being refused funds for a replacement, I gained permission to try to raise a fund specifically for the purchase of an electric organ. I wrote personal letters to all the 'children of Sherman' who had moved away. A sympathetic farmer took me round all the farms, asking for donations or promises.

Fortunately, every resident of Sherman and its neighbourhood felt the church was theirs and wanted the best for it – whether or not they were worshippers. Money came in very quickly, and I was able to purchase a Baldwin organ for 2,000 dollars – without touching church funds. So generous were the responses that I was also able to purchase an automatic music centre, and connect it to a loudspeaker on top of the church tower. On Saturday evenings and Sunday mornings I would play three vinyl records of church bells, on a clear night, they could be heard for miles around.

The success of this project was a blessing to the community, and certainly enhanced my standing as the new minister. Following a visit to the church to discuss my work, the Professor of Pastoral Care returned to the Seminary and said, "Ken, if you wanted to turn the sanctuary into a swimming pool, they'd let you!"

I didn't go for that but, after persuading the elders that the pulpit should not be between the full-length stained-glass window of Jesus and the worshippers, they allowed me to move it to the side of the platform – where it remained without question during my pastorate. However, I have to report that as soon as I left in 1960, the pulpit was restored to its former place in the centre!

The Parsonage on the eastern corner of the triangle was a large, rambling, wooden structure with a barn attached. On a cold night the joints would contract, and creak continuously, giving the impression that the house was alive. The floors were uneven, so that when we went from the bed to the bathroom, we almost ran downhill. An oil furnace in the basement provided heat, which was blown around the house through vents in every room.

Outside the garage was a large tree which I thought was in danger of falling. I was assured, with 'knowing grins', that it had been like that for years and was perfectly safe. One Friday afternoon, while I was returning from the Seminary at the end of a semester, the tree fell across the entrance to the garage! The 'all-knowing' men were embarrassed, but immediately arranged for the trunks to be cut into reasonable lengths, and I spent the next few weeks filling the barn with firewood for the winter. My wielding of the axe gave me another secure place in their acceptance as 'one of them'. The previous student minister, they said, hadn't been able to knock a nail in the wall to hang a picture.

The driveway to the Parsonage had opened on to the main road, along which large potato trucks travelled regularly. I persuaded the church to let me construct a safer driveway, opening on to the side road, using a borrowed pick and shovel, I opened the new driveway and remember being asked by a passer-by, "Ever done any manual work before?" Responding that I'd been a coal miner, I moved even closer into their acceptance.

After being given half a tree for firewood, before beginning the winter fires we wondered about the state of the chimneys. We asked the Chairman of the Business Committee whether we could have the chimneys swept. He gave us a look of complete incredulity. I'm sure he'd never before heard of the problem; there being no coal used, probably there was no soot.

Jack replied that he'd talk to Essex Smith, the captain of the local fire brigade. For a while, no more was said or heard. Then one evening, just as it was getting dark, I was returning from pastoral visiting when I saw a fire engine outside our home.

A searchlight was playing on the roof, where two men were trying to push brushes down the chimney. Whilst probably never having heard of 'sweeping a chimney', the folk had nevertheless done what they could to please these odd English people with their funny ideas! It was all done in a good spirit, proving to be another learning experience – for them and for us.

On the subject of the fire brigade, I'm reminded of an Easter morning service when the church was full, the children having to sit cross-legged all over the platform. Right in the middle of the workshop the siren sounded, indicating a fire. The voluntary fire fighters were at prayer but, at the 'call to action', each man rose instinctively and clambered over the pews towards the door – causing mayhem in the congregation. The Fire House was only 50 yards from the church, and soon the engine was on its way – with the best-dressed crew of fire fighters any emergency had ever seen! One man claimed to be wearing a brand-new suit for the Easter service.

Though the fire was in a barn at Patten, about six miles away, it was reported that the Sherman brigade got there before the locals.

Harvest Festival

I **decided to** introduce the church to another English tradition – a Harvest Festival service. We did our best to convey what such a service involves – with its flowers, fruit and vegetables in great variety. The idea was accepted, the day was arranged, and the people brought their goods for display. I believe that almost everyone brought potatoes! I remember no vegetable gardens being cultivated, and no one knew what an allotment was. But, after all, this was potato-growing country – and so the Harvest Festival duly celebrated the local harvest!

Incidentally, such was their dependence on the price of potatoes, that if they were selling for a dollar a barrel – there was gloom; if the price fetched six dollars a barrel – everyone seemed to be driving a new car!

During the potato harvest, children were allowed out

of school for three weeks, and the money earned often went towards the purchase of new clothes. Sheila and I participated in this potato picking. We would appear on the potato field early in the morning. Work would start as soon as the frost cleared from the ground, and we picked all day. A tractor digger would unearth the potatoes; we would then fill our buckets, and transfer the potatoes to a wooden barrel (this held about one and a half hundredweights) – for which we were paid 65 cents. Children and grandparents made up the harvesting team; a jovial grandmother named Bessie Martin was among the fastest and most efficient. Winters could come quickly, and be severe, so the potato harvest was the top autumn priority. We were glad to be part of it, both for the identification with the people – and the money!

During September 1958 to September 1959, Sheila's mother joined us at Sherman. She adjusted very well from the lush atmosphere of Bournemouth, and became quite enthusiastic at walking over deep snow in snow-shoes. She also made friends in Sherman, and was a companion for Sheila during her first winter. We had also acquired a lovely dog, Trixie, who was very much part of the total scene and who came with us when we moved to a new Pastorate in Utica, New York – remaining our family companion until we returned to England in 1971.

Winter

*T***he severity of** the New England winters could be a problem. In the summer we might see a hundred degrees of heat, whilst the winters regularly saw the barometer fall below zero Fahrenheit. Spring was very short. I remember going fishing on a sunny Spring day, yet when walking through the woods to the lake I had to climb over quite high snowdrifts. At the other end of the summer, the Fall could be beautiful, with a riot of colour in the trees which would often last until the end of October.

I have referred to a small building next to the Parsonage which had been the local library. Sheila had worked in Bangor Public Library for our first year in the Seminary, so the empty building presented a challenge. She requested permission from the Counsellors to explore the possibility of re-opening this highly desirable social facility. They agreed a figure of 200 dollars so she could purchase new books. The Bangor City librarian was also enthusiastic, and allowed her to transfer a thousand books from the library at Bangor to Sherman.

The building was renovated, partly by the Senior High youth group, who also replaced the leaking roof. The old books were cleaned, and some of them remained suitable for lending. An oil stove was installed for eat in the winter. Eventually, the library opened again to serve the literary needs of the Sherman folk, for which they were very grateful, and which continued long after we left.

I remember going into the library one Sunday to light the stove so that there would be sufficient warmth by Tuesday. To my dismay, the stove had leaked and oil covered the floor. Wanting it to open in time for Tuesday, I mopped up as much oil as I could – only to notice that my fingers were becoming white and wrinkled. The cold was proving too much, and I only just avoided frostbite by immersing my hands for a while in cold water.

Both winter cold and the summer heat were somewhat mitigated by the high humidity. The extremes of temperature were more bearable because of the dry atmosphere. However, we needed to be careful because, in really cold weather, the hair in the nose could freeze like little sticks, and the ears could easily become unsightly from frostbite.

On the whole, the Americans have learned to handle these climate difficulties, and accept whatever comes as being natural and inevitable. I was often amazed when families set off in their cars for long journeys, despite a lot of snow. Of course, with the snow regularly pushed to the sides of the road, the banks were high – and cars could slide into them without incurring too much damage!

We seminary students would always set off on a Friday afternoon for our student parishes (often many miles away – mine was ninety-four), because such travelling was often on icy roads. I do remember some students, concerned about the water in their car radiators, would run the engines at intervals during a Thursday night to make sure the cars were fit to drive when needed. The elements were a constant challenge, but most Americans rose to the situations without complaint or self-pity.

My first funeral service proved to be an experience I will never forget; in fact I had two on the same day. The first was to be held at the funeral parlour of the local undertaker. It was to be conducted at my discretion, and I had no warning of what to expect. I arrived at the appointed time, and talked to the Director in his kitchen. I was to move into the parlour where the family was gathered and conduct the service standing by the casket (coffin). I duly moved in, somewhat nervously, saw the casket, and took my place at the head – only to look down, find the casket open, and see a beautifully made-up, middle-aged lady lying beside me. She was in a gorgeous dress, with jewellery everywhere, and looking at least twenty years younger than I had been led to expect. I almost felt like asking her how she was doing! I don't remember much about the service, but assume I regained my composure and did what I was there for in terms of Scripture readings, prayers, and eulogistic comments.

The second service took place in a small wooden shack. I was better prepared after the first experience. The widow, Pearl Lane, became one of the best friends of both Sheila and her mother.

It may be of interest to record that, as soon as the schools broke up for the summer, the church was expected to provide two weeks of Vacation Bible School. This entailed morning and afternoon classes, with relevant activities to suit all ages. Some were held on the church premises, others in the Parsonage, or out of doors. Preparations for these were something of a nightmare in the first year because most of the leadership was expected to be provided by the Pastor and his wife. Sheila rose to the occasion magnificently, teaching them songs they could sing, new projects they could do, and new interests to keep them profitably busy. The two weeks concluded with a public service and display in the church, to which the parents came to see what we had been doing with their children.

Sherman Mills provided us with two and a half years of new experiences, and we were able to give them a few as well! After fifty years, our memories are still fresh. We often wonder where time has taken some of our young people, and we thank God for this enriching episode.

Chapter 6

Moving home

I **concluded** my theological training in May 1960 – and received the Bachelor of Divinity and Master of Divinity degrees. We'd been happy and comfortable in Sherman Mills, and were looking forward to remaining for another year. I wanted to catch up on the books I ought to have read, assess my theological stance, and have time to settle down after three demanding years. This was also the expectation of the Church.

Earlier in the year we had received an unexpected telephone call. I should explain that in Sherman the telephone system was simplistic. A square box hung on the wall – and we could only dial directly to the local exchange. The exchange, in turn, put us through to whomsoever we wished to talk (thus, the person operating the exchange was in an interesting position!).

A call came one evening. "This is Bill Williams of the Bethesda Welsh church in central New York. We're without a Minister, and have heard of you. Would you consider talking to us about the future?" I explained our position and intentions, and declined the offer.

Bill Williams was persuasive. He argued, "We're the oldest Welsh church in America. All our Ministers have come from Wales. Now the Utica City Council is going to take our building for urban redevelopment. We are 240 members. Please at least meet with us!"

Utica was 200 miles from Sherman, and I agreed to meet the Committee in Sturminster – about the halfway point. We were arranging the precise meeting place, and Bill was explaining directions, "You come down the Maine Turnpike and turn left" – at which point a voice interrupted, "No you don't, you turn right."! The telephone operator was listening to a conversation we didn't want her, or anyone else in Sherman, to know about!

We subsequently met the group in a church, and were persuaded at least to visit Bethesda in Utica to conduct a service of worship there. Following that visit we received a 'Call' to the pastorate, and had to consider how we could explain our change of plans to the folk at Sherman, and ease them into a new future.

We were fortunate in that a mature couple had come

to the Seminary, and needed a Manse and Pastorate. I therefore introduced them to the Church, where they were accepted. They arrived to take up the pastoral/preaching duties half an hour before we left for Utica!

Whilst the Church was glad there was no vacancy, I believe they felt let down. We had made no formal commitment to stay for another year, but the Church felt we'd 'given our word', and had broken it. We were sorry about this but thought that, in the circumstances, the best had happened for all concerned.

Before we left Sherman Mills era, another dramatic experience should be recorded. Sheila's mother had been with us for a year. In October 1959, she had to return to England. Her ship would be leaving Quebec at about eight o'clock one evening, but there was a complication; I had an important funeral to conduct at 2.00pm the following day.

It was a cold evening. We saw Mrs B. on the ship, and began our journey back to Sherman – about 400 miles. We knew we couldn't complete the journey, but decided to travel as far as we could. On crossing a bridge out of Quebec, the car went out of control on an icy road – and we 'proceeded' with the car going backward most of the time! However, progress was essential – so we continued carefully, hoping to reach a place called Jackman. This meant ascending a long hill, with a glassy-looking river many feet below us on our right. Driving as steadily as I could, I became aware that the tyres were skidding on the icy surface. It was the most dangerous drive we'd ever encountered, but we did eventually arrive in Jackman at about midnight.

We found a Hunter's Lodge still open, and asked for a room – only to be told, "This is the hunting season and every room is full"! In response to our appeal, the receptionist said, "Well, there's a small back room you can have for four dollars."

We accepted gladly, and were shown into the room – which seemed to be full of doors. We decided to spend a short night, and leave early so as to be back home in time for the funeral.

Starting to undress, I opened a door – thinking it was a wardrobe, only to find myself looking down at a couple in bed, less than a yard from where I was standing! I closed the door quickly, and we lay on our clothes until about 5.00am when we resumed our journey. We stopped for a roadside breakfast about 8.00am, and eventually arrived in Sherman Mills about 1.00pm – just in time to change for the funeral at 2.00pm.

I'd been attending a very sick man who lived in a small wooden shack with his wife and young family. They couldn't afford hospitalisation, so he died at home.

During the funeral service, the widow collapsed and had to be carried out of the Church. She was exhausted from caring for her husband and young family, in real poverty. Again this background, our difficulties in returning from Quebec on icy roads seemed light by comparison.

Utica

Utica is a city in the centre of New York State, 200 miles from New York City via the New York Throughway, and 200 miles from Niagara Falls (which border Canada). There were five ethnic groups in the city, each with their own churches and funeral directors, etc. To the east was a German settlement, to the west, an Italian district. There were also Polish people, people of mixed race and, finally, the Welsh. In the eighteenth century, many Welsh people had migrated to get away from poverty in Wales to work in the textile industry here.

By 1960, the largest Welsh Presbyterian Church in America was 'Moriah', known as the "Lace Curtain Welsh". The oldest (having been founded in 1803) was 'Bethesda', which had 500 members and was known as the "Shanty Welsh". All the ethnic churches gave much help when new families arrived needing accommodation and jobs.

Until 1934, no word of English had ever been heard from the Bethesda pulpit. The congregation was Welsh and proud of it (needing the language for their identity). All previous Bethesda ministers had been called directly from Wales, and preached in Welsh. I was a compromise – though Sheila and I were born in Wales, neither of us could speak Welsh.

On learning of my appointment, three families resigned in protest. Sheila was frequently asked in Woman's Group meetings, (always in an emphatic Welsh accent!) "How is it that you were born in Wales and cannot *speak* Welsh?"

In general, my appointment in 1960 was appropriate. Everyone understood English. Many members had been born in Utica, and some had fought in the American forces.

The challenges we faced in Bethesda were entirely different from those we'd encountered in Sherman Mills; in many ways they were more complex. I could fulfil the preaching/ pastoral duties as before, but Sheila couldn't find a role. The youth groups seemed to have as many leaders as young people – and, whilst we suited the younger adults, we weren't Welsh enough for the older members.

There was also the cloud of re-location hanging over the Church; at one time we were considering five different options. Some felt we were not fighting the problems sufficiently, and a few resigned over the issue. We had almost decided to purchase a beautiful Presbyterian church building known as 'Soyne Memorial' when a woman was raped on the property; no further interest was shown!

Sheila resolved her sense of loneliness by enrolling on a correspondence course with Wolsey Hall College in London. She studied Latin, English Literature and Religious Knowledge. At the end of the course, an examination was arranged in Boston – and she gained qualifications in two of the subjects.

The Welsh had retained their love of singing, and every November a local Gymanfa Ganu (singing festival) was celebrated. A conductor was brought over from Wales, and we sang the old Welsh hymns all day – even eating our meals in the church. Morih and Bethesda alternated as venues; the sanctuaries were paced with enthusiastic singers, and the event left us inspired for many days.

One year we accommodated the National Gymanfa Ganu; singers came from all over America and Canada. These were great days – when we celebrated the traditions of the past, whilst also trying to make them part of our present. Ties to the old country were interesting. During the War, parcels of food (etc) were sent to families in Wales. One story told of tea bags being included, which had gained the thankful but puzzled response, "They're lovely, but isn't it difficult to get the tea out of the bags?"!

Some immigrants, when they became more prosperous, visited Wales to learn more about their roots. They expected to return with interesting stories about their ancestors. Instead, friends often found them reluctant and evasive; what they had discovered, they preferred *not* to talk about! Many early Welsh settlers had been trying to escape their 'deeds', as well as their poverty!

In 1962, Bethesda finally decided to merge with the Plymouth church, and to name it 'Plymouth-Bethesda'. The Plymouth minister had resigned, so the pulpit was vacant. At first, I was to be Interim Minister – with a decision to be made later about my role. Almost all the Bethesda members transferred to the merged church, thereby creating a total membership of 800.

Developments on the national scene tended to help the uniting of the congregations. Race riots and violence were increasing in frequency. Martin Luther King was shot – shortly after telling a spell-bound America of his *Dream* – "I have a dream, that one day …"

In 1963, came the shock of President J.F. Kennedy's

assassination, followed by that of his brother Robert. These events overshadowed any difficulties in the merger process. We held many special days for prayer and concern about the nation. These events also raised questions about American policies. Most people trusted the President, and almost felt that "America can do no wrong."

Others were beginning to wonder how many of our troubles had been created by foolish decisions in the top-level policy making. If I raised such a concern, I might be told, "Don't you criticise our President. If you don't like what we're doing, you can always go home." A highly respected Sunday School leader said to Sheila, "I guess we're Americans first, and Christians second."

With thousands of other Protestant ministers I was becoming increasingly 'protestant' about American actions and, because of my position in the Church and city, we decided to become U.S. citizens.

The Ecumenical Movement

*I*n this national context, and with many pastoral calls, I quickly found my place. Early one Sunday I had to visit a home where a husband had died, leaving a widow and four children under fifteen. During the morning worship I received a baby in baptism. Later in the afternoon a couple came to see me about a wedding in the local hospital, and a baby was born to the lady who sensed she may be more American than Christian. All this happened in one day, a Palm Sunday.

Another national development was the Ecumenical movement. In the early sixties, Pope John decided "to open the windows of the Roman Catholic Church and let in some fresh air."

The response among American clergy was delight and enthusiasm. With the oldest Monsignor, I called an ecumenical committee in my Church, and everyone seemed glad to break down barriers and begin joint activities immediately. Protestant ministers preached in Roman Catholic pulpits, and vice versa.

During the first Week of Prayer for Christian Unity (17–24 January), united services of worship were held every night to packed congregations – despite temperatures falling well below zero. I preached at one service in a Catholic church – with the attendance cited in the newspaper report of 850. During the first 'Thanksgiving' in the ecumenical era, we rented the local ice hockey auditorium and attracted 6000 worshippers. I still have pictures and newspaper clippings covering these events. It was an exciting time to be in the Christian ministry – though, by way of contrast, there was increasing gloom over the Vietnam War and racial disturbances.

Throughout our ministry we've been very fortunate with our living conditions. In Maine we lived in a house, supplied with free electricity, in the centre of the community. A local farmer tithed his home-grown winter provisions and gave us a chest-freezer full of lamb and other farm produce – in all about 32 packages of good organic food.

In Utica we enjoyed a four-storey house, at the edge of the city. It was near a long ski tow and wooded hill – at the bottom of which was a park and an open air ice rink where children could play. Later, when we came to Castle Green Church in Bristol (England), a manse had been purchased in the 'highly desirable area' of Thingwall Park, Fishponds. Again we found ourselves at the edge of a city, with long views of the countryside and a large allotment site almost on the doorstep. Here we enjoy very friendly neighbours with well-behaved children. We know there is a wide variety of help available, should we have any emergency needs, and constantly remind ourselves of these privileges and are grateful for them.

The churches we have served provided us with resources and challenges. In Maine, ours was the only church, hence there was no competition or religious tension. The people were friendly, co-operative, and willing for us to try any experiments in the early days of our ministry.

For the most part, the Bethesda congregation accepted us as part of the Welsh tradition (though we couldn't speak Welsh). Like any family, we faced together the inevitable transitions of increasing age and challenges in our circumstances. The Plymouth church building was a large, relatively modern complex in a prominent position on the outskirts of Utica, with a good cross-section of Welsh/Americans. The church consisted of 560 members, a full-time secretary and custodian; there was also an Associate Minister, who had a ministerial background or appropriate experience in social skills. At the merger in 1963, the combined membership rose to 800.

For the first year, I was the Interim Minister. The money Bethesda brought from the sale of its buildings meant we were a wealthy church. Some Plymouth members realised that, with so many advantages, they could search the country for the best minister available to fill the vacant pulpit. It was perfectly understandable, because I was relatively inexperienced. I was also regarded by those who remembered the 1883 breakaway from Bethesda (when the congregation wanted to be fully American) as too much associated with Welsh traditions.

Tensions were inevitable, and soon a pulpit committee was formed to resolve them. While they were considering many potential candidates, and surreptitiously visiting churches where ministers were known to want a move, I did the pastoral and preaching work and tried to respond as creatively as I could to the challenges of the situation. Eventually, the committee decided to recommend my permanent appointment but, even on the Sunday when they were due to vote, a small group canvassed people as they came to the church; "Let's get this Welshman out of our pulpit!" I think I received about 75% of the vote. Some friends assured me that, in the circumstances, this was good. With the resolution of the leadership issue behind us, we all settled down to the work of the church.

My protests against the war in Vietnam continued, and I learned all I could about the facts and figures. I was asked to take part in an hour-long debate on radio – with a Presbyterian minister and an Army Officer speaking *for* the war whilst a lawyer and I argued *against*. The broadcast took place on a Sunday afternoon from 2.00-3.00pm, and was chaired by the President of the Ecumenical Group.

Between the morning service and the radio broadcast a Trustee of Plymouth-Bethesda took me aside and said, "Ken, if you go ahead with this today, I will not answer for your future in this Church. You could lose your job, and your home."

I replied "E; there are some things a person must do out of conscience, whatever the cost." Following the broadcast, there was a general silence from church members and friends.

Then one man came to the Manse and said, "Ken, we may not agree with your stance on the war, but we recognise you were the best informed person in the debate."

Body bags continued to arrive back in the States, and more and more radio and T.V. commentators raised questions and showed pictures of the horrors suffered by the soldiers in the field. There was also a creeping fear that we weren't winning the easy victory we'd been promised; on the contrary, there were politically motivated excuses for strategic retreats. Eventually, defeat was tacitly acknowledged, and America suffered a serious blow to its confidence as a world power.

As in any very large congregation, dramatic and humorous things often happened. I used to visit a wealthy doctor (Dr H.) who'd made a fortune on the Stock Exchange. I conducted his wife's funeral; she lay in a casket thought to be worth over 5,000 dollars. About a year later the doctor himself died, and left the church 15% of his estate (thought to be worth about 7 million). He also left me 5,000 dollars. Molly, my secretary, thought it should have been more! Following these 'disclosures', she telephoned the doctor's housekeeper about the legacies. She reported "it was because Revd Roach always had clean, shiny shoes when he came" that the doctor had decided to leave me the money! With it we were able to pay off the mortgage on our house in Bournemouth, where our widowed mothers were now living in separate apartments.

The Dr H legacy to the church amounted to almost one million dollars – yet another challenge of Christian responsibility and practical wisdom. I suggested that if the money was not used wisely the gift could do us more harm than good. The congregation was divided into four main Boards, each with many sub-committees. There was Board of Deacons for the spiritual life; a Board of Trustees for buildings (etc); a Board for Christian Education and Youth Work; and a Board for Mission Outreach (of which Sheila was a member).

I offered as an ideal that for every dollar we spent on our own church we should give a dollar to some kind of mission enterprise – local or international. This principle was accepted – and we agreed that the Board for Missions should administer half the legacy. Generous gifts were soon being distributed, and good causes financed, such as supplying major encyclopaedias and books for a library in the Coloured community. We also sent a generous cheque to the Bangor Theological Seminary where I felt I'd received a very good training and practical support.

Friends

Another important aspect of my ministry was the series of denominational mergers. In 1931, the Evangelical denomination in the U.S. merged with the Reformed and, three years later, the Congregationalists merged with the 'Christian' movement.

In 1961, I was a delegate in Philadelphia when those four former denominations came together to form the United Church of Christ. In 1972, I was a delegate in London for the merging of the Presbyterian Church with the Congregational Church in England and Wales, thus forming the United Reformed Church.

Throughout our ministry in the Plymouth-Bethesda Church we were much supported by the friendship of the D. family. This was of strategic benefit because Mr D was a vocal man on the board of Trustees – whilst Mrs D. was active and involved in several area of the Church's life. At one time she was the Church Moderator and, therefore, the Chairperson of the Executive Council which represented the four Boards and all the Committees. There were five children in the D. family – each of them academic, and potential leaders. All this was particularly helpful because they were part of the 'Plymouth side' of the merged congregation. Not only did they approve of what we were trying to do in the Pastorate, but they also became our closest family friends.

We spent a lot of time in each other's houses. Interestingly, we were not in the same camp politically so, tactfully, we never discussed the issue of the Vietnam War or my involvement in the protests. There was a mutual respect for differences even on this vital matter, and it protected the relationship from tensions and division. Later, when we adopted two babies, the D. family became our extended family; their support was invaluable in every way (especially as we had no relatives in the U.S.A).

Alongside the challenges and difficulties in our situation were also occasions of fun and hilarity. I shall never forget a lady called Linda Gleeson. She was eccentric, rather loud, but colourful – always a unique individual. She like to think of herself as girlish, and wanted to be known as Luidi. She lived not far from us with her sister. Both women were unmarried. Living above them was a

Welsh couple, who kept a parental eye on their affairs.

Luidi was taken ill, and died after a short illness. Each church had its own funeral director, but Luidi had requested that she be buried from the German Funeral Home run by a family called Kunkels.

This was a big surprise to the Williams Funeral Home, which invariably catered for the Welsh-Congregational members.

Before the funeral itself, 'Calling Hours' were available during the afternoons and evenings so that families and friends could view the body and pay their respects. Each Director specialised in embalming skills, and regularly made a body in the casket look twenty years younger than in life.

On this occasion the Kunkels wanted to do their best work with Luidi in order to impress the Welsh-American folk who would be paying their respects. Consequently, Luidi was in her most colourful dress – with all her jewellery on display and a hair-do which was 'out of this world'! She'd never looked better – and it was the hair-do that made the biggest impression. The Kunkels had excelled, and many visitors to the Funeral Home commended that Williams Bros. now had a serious competitor for their 'last rites' services!

I conducted the service there, after which we proceeded to a new cemetery where conditions had been imposed to make "The Crown" the best in the city. There would be no ugly gravestones; no decaying flowers would be left; only two bodies would be allotted to any one grave. When Luidi was finally laid to rest, in a new grave purchased for herself and her sister, the casket was lowered to a depth of about eight feet. I remember feeling a bit shocked at the depth, but room had to be allowed for her sister when she died.

Some time later I was planting bulbs in my front garden when I became aware of a cyclist coming around the corner, apparently heading for our house; I recognised B;N;, the man living above the sisters and in charge of their affairs. He looked agitated as he headed straight for my garden.

"Reverend," he said, "We're in big trouble."

I tried to be calm, assuring him that together we could deal with whatever had happened. With shaking hands, he produced an impressive looking envelope. "I've had this letter from the most elitist Mail-order Company in America. This is what it says 'Dear Miss Gleeson. Please send us a cheque immediately, or return the expensive wig you ordered on approval.'"

He looked at me wildly, "But Reverend, you buried her in it; you buried her in it!" Luidi had the last laugh – even at the end; it all seemed to fit the picture of her we'd known so well.

A Family of Four

*S*ummers in America can get very hot, with the cities both stifling and oppressive. Therefore many families purchased a chalet-style 'camp' on a site out in the country – often beside a lake. We were fortunate in having such a site – Trenton Assembly Park, owned by the Methodist church – sixteen miles north of Utica. We had purchased a two-storey wooden structure; There were about forty camps on the site, with a chapel in the centre. There was also a natural swimming pool, fed by a river – a pipe brought water in, and an outlet back to the river kept the level constant at all times.

Most families moved to the camps shortly after the schools broke up for the summer holiday, and returned after Labour Day (the first Monday in September). The men could commute to their work, and the mothers had a safe, healthy place to occupy their children. Screened windows protected against insects, as well as allowing air to circulate. Benches and tables outside provided pleasant eating facilities. The summer camps are a real feature of American life, and help to solve the problems of hot summer days and airless nights.

Every Sunday afternoon the campsite would be quiet between two and three o'clock whilst a service of worship was held for anyone interested; Cars being driven into the site were restricted to five miles an hour. Telephones and radios enabled families to keep in touch with the outside world It was all very practical and ideal – both for the families and for entertaining visitors.

Shortly before we purchased our camp we had embarked on another major life-changing development. We'd been married for ten years, with no sign of children. We decided to apply for adoption. The sexual revolution of the 'sixties meant that many babies were available, so our application was warmly welcomed. The process of ensuring suitability was going through smoothly. Our social status in the Church was highly respected. Three sponsors gladly supported our application, and the Children's Department of the Social Services assured us that, in due course, we could have a lovely baby who would fit into our family perfectly.

Towards the end of one interview, I made a casual

remark. I told the lady we were not American citizens. The atmosphere froze; she changed character completely. "What d'you mean, asking for an American child if you are not American? You should have known that no alien can adopt a baby in this country! Why've you been wasting our time?"

Then a change of expression came over her face and, breaking the silence, she said, "Well, anyway, leave it with me."

So we let the office, at about noon, and returned home very crestfallen. Interestingly, we'd never even thought about seeking citizenship for the purpose of adoption.

About five o'clock the phone rang. "This is the Social Services Department – have you given us an interesting day! We rang the main city office; they hadn't heard of the problem. A further call to the New York State office in Albany brought the same response. Finally, we telephoned Washington D.C." – who had promptly referred the question to Robert Kennedy (then the Attorney General to his brother President J. F. Kennedy).

It is Robert Kennedy who recommended that our adoption application should proceed! We're probably the first non-Americans to have adopted an American child.

In due course a lovely three-month old baby girl was given to us on a six-month approval basis. She was a secure, smiling baby who slept soundly, and had obviously enjoyed her first three months in a foster home. A photograph received with the foster home notes shows her laughing and kicking on a sofa (which was badly worn – suggesting a materially poor house). The teenage mother had, sadly, been obliged to give her up at birth, but the loving foster care had evidently compensated for the separation from the natural parent.

After six months we secured the full legal adoption and changed the baby's name to 'Alison'. The church and our friends were delighted, and she was baptised the Sunday after our official confirmation to the Pastorate of Plymouth-Bethesda early 1964.

Just over a year later we applied to adopt a second baby girl. By now we had decided to become American citizens – in order to be in a better position to oppose the Vietnam War. The application for citizenship went through quickly, and we were made full Americans in July 1964.

We were delighted in 1965 a second baby became available. She had not been so fortunate in her first three months. She had had several foster homes, and the day we brought her home from one we noticed there were five babies in cots, side by side. There was a sad, but revealing, sentence in the accompanying notes, "This child feeds better if held."

We could have cried. Surely a baby needs to be held and cuddled, especially when being fed. We imagined the babies having a bottle of milk put in their mouths, then, perhaps, a bottle rolling out on the floor – without the loss being noticed.

When we gave Hilary (as she became) a bottle of milk, she would literally guzzle it down, as if she had to drink it whilst she could. Initially, she couldn't sleep for more than twenty minutes at a time – usually waking up shaking and screaming. She was obviously very insecure, and we reported out concerns to the Children's Department. They assured us that she was perfectly normal, and would respond completely to the love and attention of a good home.

Fortunately, within a few weeks, Sheila was able to take both children to live in our summer camp. There we had help with the care of Alison, whilst Sheila gave that constant love and attention so needed by our second baby. Hilary loved lying in a pram looking up at the overhanging branches. She responded quickly to the fresh air, good food, and leisurely attention we were better able to give there than whilst living in the city. When we returned home in September, we knew we were taking a very different child from the one we had received in June. Improvements on every front were enjoyed by all and, by the end of the year, another legal adoption was complete. We were now a normal happy family of four.

The 'big family' nature of the Church was a real help, with the D. friends acting as close extended family. Sheila could bring the children to join me for lunch in the Church, after which they could play in the Games Room. This brought us all together for the mid-day meal, and gave Sheila a break from the house. That was especially welcome in the winter months. The Manse was only about half a mile from the Church, an easy, level walk.

The Church also provided an excellent Sunday School for all ages, including a well-run nursery section. Later, the children enjoyed the weekday provisions there. These were well equipped and staffed, partly from the proceeds of the Dr. H. legacy. Whilst missing our natural extended family to help with the care of the children, our close friends and the Church family made the total situation easier and were totally supportive.

As the children grew older, and with my tenure of the Pastorate due to be reviewed, our future became an increasing concern. I was forty-one when we adopted Alison. This meant that as my earning capacity would be lessening, the cost of raising and educating the girls would be rising. In America, High School concluded at

18 years of age – but a further four years in college was normal for everyone who expected to make something of their lives.

Education was expensive, and most families had to make huge sacrifices to meet the bills, often getting into debt for many years. All this was taken for granted, and most people felt we were fortunate to be in a country where there were so many opportunities for anyone prepared to work for them. I had made an enquiry about a move to another church but, because theological students were exempt from Call-up duties, there was a surplus of ministers – especially at my salary level.

I'd been in Utica for eleven years, a seven years tenure was considered about right for an efficient ministry. There was also the matter of our two widowed mothers getting older, and possibly needing more supervised care. After careful consideration of all the issues, we decided to return to England and, in May 1971, we booked a berth on the *QE2*.

As a result of this decision, we experienced yet another example of American generosity. We received a 'phone call from a man in New York city who said, "I've heard you're going back to England. You've been good to my brother (B. Owen), and I want to offer you a week's holiday in my apartment – or in any New York hotel of your choice."

We didn't know New York, and didn't fancy trying to live with two small children for a week in an upper class apartment, so we asked for his recommendation – and then agreed to be accommodated in the Hotel Roosevelt on Fifth Avenue.

The week proved to be an ideal holiday before resuming life in England. I don't remember much of what we did, but the affluence of the hotel certainly impressed us greatly. We walked around a number of famous areas, including Greenwich Village – known for its Bohemian lifestyle. We didn't like what we saw, and soon returned to more normal city life. However, it was an awesome experience to wander around under skyscrapers and to visit such important places as the United Nations building.

Mr Owen not only paid all the expenses, he also gave us 'pocket money'. Our last contact with him was when he visited us in our cabin on board the *QE2*. His life couldn't have all luxury and ease – because I remember one of his comments, "Mr Roach, there is no peace in this world."

America has been a focus of world attention, fear and envy for many years. It has been amazing growth in its two hundred years history. As a young country, with enormous resources, it has grown in wealth and military power. Our experience of its generosity reflects a people who have opened their borders to countless refugees from every nation of the world. It has also welcomed millions who wanted to realise their potential and make a better life for their families.

In turn, many immigrants have made enormous contributions to the general life of the U.S.A. Some have given guidance to the political areas, others to education, religious thinkers have certainly found the freedom and opportunities they need to enrich their respective philosophical and religious fields. We benefitted from a theological education we couldn't afford in England and from many experiences that are more possible in a young country.

Of course, every young person and country makes mistakes – but they can also learn from those mistakes. Some mistakes have come from idealism and the awareness of their ability to right some of the wrongs in the world. The foundations of the American Constitution are very idealistic – and religious, in the best sense of the word. Yet, in a country with so much religious input, they established separation of Church and State.

That boundaries have been breaking down is the reason for many misgivings about U.S. developments in our times. One example is the influence of the Fundamentalist Baptists on Presidential election. Further causes include the shock of 9/11 and other terrorist attacks. The basic trust Americans have always placed in their government is faltering. Two thirds have withdrawn their support for George Bush, and at least one Senator has admitted that many in authority "go to bed every night weeping over the state of their country."

More and more books and articles are being published and are critical of the Bush administration and its corruption, as well as over the war in Iraq. The Justice Department has publicly affirmed that law is still the foundations of American life, and that every person from a log cabin to the White House is liable to scrutiny and to be brought to justice.

So there are signs that some Americans, seeing what has been happening, are beginning to recover their national health – demanding accountability and justice from everyone in authority, right up to the White House.

We have mixed feelings about our dual citizenship, but follow news from the States with keen interest and believe that the basic idealism of America will yet triumph, and that we can again be proud of its contribution to world peace and prosperity.

An incident on board the *QE2* may be of interest. We had dined extremely well in the Roosevelt Hotel, and the ship's steward was requesting our order for food.

He looked at Hilary, aged six. She replied, very simply, "Could I just have cheese on toast, please?"!

Castle Green, Bristol

*I*n **preparation for** our return to England, I'd answered an advertisement for a job in a London adoption agency. My cousin Eric had alerted the Castle Green Congregational Church in Bristol of my availability as a minister. Their pulpit had been vacant for two years. On arrival in Bournemouth, to our relief, we were greeted with a letter offering an appointment in London *and* an invitation to be interviewed by Castle Green!

We berthed in Southampton on 18th May. On Saturday 20th, mother and I attended a family wedding in Bristol. The next day, I attended a service at Castle Green Church. A month later, I preached in Castle Green with a view to the Pastorate and, after the usual Congregational consultations, I was 'called' to the pulpit. (I had been offered the London adoption agency job, but felt very deeply that my life was still, essentially, a pilgrimage from coalpit to pulpit).

The transition from the New York church to Bristol was made easier by yet another expression of American realism and generosity. We'd been given an amazing farewell party in Plymouth-Bethesda church, and I still have a sheaf of inspiring letters from many leaders of the Catholic as well as Protestant churches in Utica. Then the church surprised me with the following information; apart from the many gifts of appreciation, they would give me a week's salary for every year of my ministry among them. I was given a sum equal to three months salary, which exactly covered our expenses from the time we arrived in Southampton in May until my induction in Castle Green in September.

I am recording those reminiscences with profound appreciation for my many blessings, and hope that I can continue to repay something for the support, encouragement and generosity I've received.

Chapter 7

England

*M*y **return to** England in 1971 to the Castle Green Congregational Church in Bristol was a re-introduction to familiar ground. My parents had almost certainly worshipped in that Church the day after their wedding. My father's sister, Annie Painter, had been the secretary of the Sisterhood for over 35 years, and the Painter family was at the heart of most of the Church's activities. As a boy, I had always attended Castle Green whilst on holiday in Bristol, and I was present at the Service of Thanksgiving celebrating the end of the war in 1945. Castle Green is one of the oldest Congregational churches in England. It began its life on the green of the old Castle in about 1613. The members were among the first Dissenters from the Established Church of England, and its first minister was imprisoned for his non-conformity. After 40 years, the congregation split into Baptists and Congregational affiliations.

The Baptists remained in the Broadmead area of the city. Two and a half centauries later, the Congregationalists moved with many of the people to a suburb known as Greenbank. Here a large building was erected in 1902, and we often heard the story of the organ being transported from the old Church on a horse-drawn cart. The challenge mush have been there, or their optimism very high, because they built a sanctuary for worship able to seat 1,000 people. During the 1930s and 40s, most of the seats would be occupied – and on special anniversaries every pew might be full.

Despite the previous minister having moved away in 1969, the church was quite strong when we arrived in 1971. Two halls and a kitchen had been added to the side of the sanctuary. There were strong youth groups for all ages, each with excellent leaders. It was not unusual at the Women's Bright Hour (which still meets on Thursday afternoons) for a hundred or more women to attend this really bright occasion of worship – with its 'happy Thoughts', refreshments, and mutual sharing. Many of the women lived alone, and the church activities must have made a great contribution to the quality of their lives and to their mental health.

A similar women's meeting, the Sisterhood, met on

Sunday afternoons. Later, a Men's Interest Group was started (this continues to meet once a month). Two related families oversaw the Boys' Brigade – and many of the boys, together with girls from the Brownies and Guides, were present at the Family Service on Sunday mornings.

We very much appreciated returning to one English tradition – the Sunday evening service. The first time I led one in Castle Green, I estimate there were 130 n the congregation. When we went to America in 1957, we found that evening services had ceased; the Junior and Senior High youth groups occupied the church buildings from 6.30pm to 9.00pm. Back in England, we once again enjoyed being able to sing the great evening hymns, such as *At even 'ere the sun was set*, and *The day Thou gavest, Lord, is ended*.

There was something so right about concluding the Sabbath with a service of appropriate hymns and quiet reflections. They served to prepare us all spiritually for the daily demands of the week ahead, as well as committing to God's mercy the mistakes or failures of the week just concluded.

I was aware of the adjustments that would have to be made, and I also knew that a minister should be both wise and cautious before trying to introduce changes in his new Pastorate. A Moderator in New York used to recommend, "Don't even try to change the air in the Sanctuary for two years!"

My Pastorate in Plymouth-Bethesda was an excellent example of *organisation*. Castle Green, in contrast, seemed to have nothing like this (except the elected Elders, and individuals responsible for various jobs). I therefore decided to try to bring in some structure to the organisation of the congregation, and obtained agreement to the idea from the Elders and church Meeting. I remember trying to set up committees for Pastoral Care, and Social Outreach – and for practical issues such as Buildings and Finance. I simply wanted more lay involvement in the decision-making processes of the Church.

The Committee structures were duly set up under the leaders recognised in the respective fields. I soon became aware that things were not working as well as I had hoped; eventually, I asked one of the leaders how his Committee was doing.

He replied, "Oh, I haven't called them together yet; I've nothing to tell them!"

It must be said, however, that he was a very good man in his field, and totally dedicated to the Church. His wife told me that R's first love was Castle Green

Church; second, was his job; third, his home! I suppose I was foolish to try to make such changes before being sure I knew the situation in the Church – or before the Church got to know me. There were obviously still many adjustments to be made by the 'old' Church – and the new Pastor!

We also had the problem of two young children having to adjust to a different school system. At six and eight years of age, the girls had to go to separate schools. This meant escorting each of them both ways, and trying to help them with the very different educational methods. Neighbours were helpful, and these duties were also shared with a Methodist Minister's family who lived nearby.

Later, we were able to arrange for both girls to go to a boarding school in Bournemouth. This had been set up a century earlier for the daughters of Congregational Ministers. Here, Alison and Hilary spent five very happy years, and benefitted from the academic standards as well as the social context. This arrangement was also convenient in that both Sheila's mother and my mother were still living in Bournemouth, so our fortnightly visits became joint family occasions. Over many years our house there served as a resource place – for the older and younger generations, as well as for ourselves.

I have reason to believe that my pulpit work and pastoral care at Castle Green were appreciated. We also initiated a ministry where, after Sunday evening services, eight members would come to the Manse for a get-together in the front room (which was suitably warmed by a coal fire). Two couples with cars would each invite two 'single' members, so that transport was assured. It worked very well; over the years I believe that every member enjoyed this conclusion to the Sabbath at least once; some especially the car owners, more often. Such evenings involved pleasant reminiscing, as well as problem-sharing opportunities, and proved to be a major contribution to pastor/ people relationships. Sheila always prepared tasty refreshments to be enjoyed in the cheerful warmth of the fireplace.

After some years of concentrated pastoral activities, I agreed to take on some District Council and Provincial responsibilities, and also enjoyed broadcasting on Radio Bristol's "Sunday Starts" programme. I became the Free Church Chaplain at 'Glenside', the local psychiatric hospital, for a period of ten years. All these contributed to my overall ministry – though some members disagreed with my acceptance of these extra tasks, and their inevitable demands on my time and energy.

At a time when the membership was aging and

declining, the work of ministers was seen as important for both the present and future of the churches. Castle Green, in common with the great majority of Congregational churches, became part of the United Reformed Church (URC) when it was formed in 1972. In the URC, when a Minister leaves a Pastorate, another Minister provides oversight in what is called an Interim Moderator arrangement. Such a church might be six miles away from one's own – thus involving extra travelling, as well as time spent chairing their meetings, doing their pastoral duties (e.g. weddings and funerals), and engaging in the search for a new Minister and arranging her or his Induction.

Once again Sheila had to accept different challenges and roles. Because my stipend was low, she needed to find paid work; fortunately, someone introduced her to the medical librarian at Frenchay Hospital. Sheila went there, part-time, in 1972. The library then consisted of little more than a collection of relevant books in a room next to a doctor's office. Later, the senior librarian proceeded to build this up so that, eventually, it became one of the best in the area. The hospital also had a patient's library, and one for nurses. The job provided Sheila with new friends and interests, as well as influence in an important social institution.

Added to her many activities in the Church, Sheila also became a lay preacher – and served many churches in this capacity over several years. She would not accept the position of President of the Woman's Bright Hour but was, nevertheless, recognised as a resource person; indeed, she was deeply involved in every area of the Church's life.

Sundays were demanding. They began with my taking a service at Glenside Hospital at 9.00am, followed by the Family Service in Castle Green at 10.30am. Sheila always tried to attend the Sisterhood at 3.00pm and the Evening Service followed this at 6.30pm. Then we entertained at home until about 10.00pm!

The weekly Prayer Meeting had stopped before I came to Bristol – but I conducted Bible Classes for ten years, which were well attended and lively. For the first two years we went through the Bible to get a bird's eye view of the whole, after which we studied one New Testament book in depth during each winter session. I do remember one winter, however, when we studied the book of Job; to our surprise, we had more laughs than one would expect from a book usually associated with a man in misery.

In 1983 the Plymouth-Bethesda Church marked the centenary of the Plymouth American Congregationalists breaking away from the Welsh Bethesda Church that had been founded in 1802. Such was the generosity of the church that they invited our whole family back for the celebrations – paying all expenses, even including the taxi service to and from Heathrow.

In 1984, I accepted the Presidency of the Ecumenical Committee in Bristol – and was privileged to help to lead a group of Roman Catholic and Protestant Christians on a pilgrimage to the Holy Land. Once more Sheila and I had 'all expenses paid'. We spent a week with 63 others walking where Jesus had walked, trying to recapture what had happened in each place – and how that might help us to live as his followers in the 20th century. I remember feeling especially close to the Master as we sailed on the Sea of Galilee. I conducted a meditation on the boat, taking the theme of how Jesus might help us to still the storms of life. Ironically – the day was hot, and the sea dead calm!

After each day's exploring, we concluded the evening meal with a devotional service conducted by an Anglican Archdeacon, The Catholic Precentor of Clifton Cathedral, or myself as representative of the Free Churches. The tour brought many of the Gospel stories to life, and stimulated some new phases in my preaching.

CHAPTER 8

RETIREMENT

*W*hilst I have had a long ministry since Ordination in 1960, the three main Pastorates (Sherman Mills, Utica, and Castle Green) each offered different and distinctive challenges. They provided me with a wide range of experiences and, hopefully, a continuous deepening of my spiritual life.

Alison and Hilary completed their education in Bournemouth, and then proceeded to further education in colleges in Bristol before finding employment in secretarial and social work posts respectively. They each married and set up homes and are still, like most of their contemporaries, grappling with the complex challenges of personal needs and family involvements as they try to find their niche in an ever-changing society.

After fourteen years in Castle Green, I decided to retire

at the age of 64. The URC had set up accommodation standards for manses, which ours now failed to meet; so the house was up for sale. Normally a minister should not retire and remain in the manse, but since there was about a mile between Church and Manse – plus a major road separating the Greenbank and Fishponds districts – it was considered acceptable for us to purchase the property. Our mothers had moved out of the house in Bournemouth, so we sold that and purchased the old Manse in Bristol – where we continue to live.

At the time of writing, I am approaching 20 years in retirement. I have remained active in conducting Sunday Services in a variety of churches of different denominations. I also undertook (part-time) the pastoral work of the URC Church in Whitchurch for a period of about three years – until transient ischemic attacks meant I could no longer drive a car. These mini-strokes also stopped my preaching for a while, but as they became less, and eventually disappeared, I resumed conducting worship services.

I've always enjoyed this – not only for the occasions themselves, but also for the challenges of preparing sermons, prayers, and choosing hymns appropriate to the current events and my understanding of the spiritual needs of modern people. I have a graphic ideal that a preacher should be equally at home with a Bible in one hand – and a good newspaper in the other!

As a balance to the desk work involved, I have cultivated an allotment for over 30 years; the exercise and fresh air there, and my other continuing interests, have helped to keep up the level of good health I'm still enjoying. Of course, the fresh organic food has also contributed – but I regard this activity, and the companionship of fellow gardeners as very important, and will continue to cultivate a plot for as long as I can. Apart from the ever-changing demands of family life – I continue to read books, keep up with the current affairs, and listen to classical music. I've also become increasingly involved in the local Anglican Church situated only five minutes' walk from our house.

During my long life I have witnessed, and been involved in, many radical changes at every level; from the primitive beginnings in rural Wales to the sophisticated advantages of modern inventions; from the narrow mental confines of Fundamentalist Pentecostalism to the ever-widening spheres of Liberal Theology and Inter-Faith; and, of course, from the deep coalpit to many pulpits.

It's been an interesting journey – and it is still going on!

Postscript

𝒟**ad wrote** his memoir quite some time ago, and since his passing I've felt it was such a waste to go unpublished. The reasons are two fold really, one for history sake and two out of respect to a wonderful husband, father and friend to many.

I would like to share with you the following: Dad stopped preaching when he turned 90, he also stopped the allotment that same year. About a year later he stopped going to the supermarket with his friend and I picked up the grocery shop. Life seemed to stand still, Dad was worried about what the future held, books and music no longer captured his imagination and interest, many days he would be 'meditating', gradually he became more unstable but still managed to walk with dignity, he hated the thought of using a stick, but managed the stairs and still had good strong hands.

"I think I feel my age," was a favourite quote.

On Tuesday 10th September 2019 at approximately 10.30pm Dad passed away (aged 97), listening to *Land of my Fathers* sung by the Welsh Male Voice Choir.

I held his hand and listening to the steady rhythm of his breathing, and thought, how long could this lovely dignified man continue? Thoughts of his Welsh roots, the recent passing of his brother, and Mum's heart attack the previous week, his love of the allotment, music, how as a child we use to walk hand in hand when taking the dog for walks and in the last year how I use to shave his tender face knowing that he loved our special time together. Tears gently flowed.

I had brought my bible with me and thought that I'd start at the beginning and see how far we got, I soon became aware of how tedious my voice must sound and remembered I had my phone with me. I message my husband, my sister, my children, my cousin and mum and dad's closest friend and thought I wondered what music I could play, both he and mum loved the Welsh Male Voice Choir – I googled and the first song started to play, I became aware his breathing changed, a big sigh and a slight flutter of a squeeze. I played another, *Myfanwy,* and flicked back to *Land of my Fathers*. I became aware the breathing had stopped, he was still, I hugged him hard, willing myself the strength to be brave, I kissed his still warm face and told him I loved him. I then let him go, I told the nurses, not wanting to use the word 'died', and then went to the next ward to inform Mum and bring her down to say her last farewell (she had visited earlier at 7pm – ironic really, both of them being in hospital).

My sister, who has been my companion and friend since childhood, supported the idea of publishing and wanted to add that he "was a lovely spiritual man. I loved him and respected him. He had a strong moral code which he brought into every part of his life. He would light up the room when he smiled and sung loudly at the top of his voice. Loved by many."

We miss you Dad.

For Mum, she bides her time, waiting to join him. Life is not ideal and she is determined to stay in their home despite the loneliness and her increasing disability. She said, "I still talk to him, sitting in that chair" – so Dad, you are still a source of comfort and stability in these crazy days.

*Dad, always expressive with his hands –
great, strong and yet elegant hands – surrounded by
his books and music*

Appendix

A Poem:
Be still and know that I am God
(Ps 46:10)

Be still and know that I am God
Pure salt and light and mountain breath *(Matthew 5:13)*
We are much more than we can 'know'
Eternal life, as well as earthly sod.

Be still and know the love divine
That cares as Mother for a child. *(Hosea 11:1-4)*
That's patient, warm and kindly wise
and wants our real self to grow.

Be still and know the Joy that's more than pleasure
That stays when happiness has gone
That holds the centre of life's wheel together
Which inner glory is life's finest Treasure.

Be still and know God's perfect peace
Beyond all understanding
That is above our moods and powers
And bids the storms of life to cease.

Be still and know the kind of Rest
That is the Mystic's art;
That heals our bruised and troubled souls
And is a 'spring of water' in the heart.

Be still and know the Truth that sets us free
That ever IS ... however much we doubt
That lives while human theories die
God's truth in Christ can make us truly free.

Be still and know the Presence in our being
That made Creation by His Word
That is our strength for daily living
And aim of all our thought and seeing.

Be still and know that creeping dark will stop our play
When runs and scores are added up.
"You've had your innings" as they say
But life's true game is
Endless light and day.

Rev. K. E. Roach, 2009

A Meditation

It's very quiet now
Everything is so fresh, so pure
So charged with life, with real life, no longer imagined.
So still, so restful, stillness, rest,
Into more life
Into reconciliation
Into wholeness and at-one-ment
Into the deep, deep peace of God.

Floating, floating, like a white bird on the water
Floating unresisting, effortless
Between the real and the imagined
Between what comes to me from outside and what wells up
from deep, deep, down within me.

Floating unresisting, without effort on the surface of the
great flowing river of life, smooth, silent river.
Floating so still, so silently, that it seems to be asleep, not
flowing at all, still sleeping river, flowing irresistibly.
Flowing inevitably, silently, irrevocably into
an ever-fuller life
Into a living peace, so profound, so rich.
Because in it all my strivings, all my sorrows are taken into
its own stillness and peace.

It is into that stillness, into that peace that I am now moving, floating.
Just floating, not doing anything, just letting go
Just allowing myself to be carried along
Just letting this irresistible sleeping river take me where it is going;
Knowing all the time, that is where I want to go, where I have to go;
Into more life, into reconciliation
Into worldliness, into at-one-ment
Into living peace.

Rev. K. E. Roach

Printed in Great Britain
by Amazon